at the time of the shipwreck in Cardigan Bay. Superintendent Jones is in communication with the relatives on the matter.

RED WHARF BAY.

THE LATE MR J. JONES.—The funeral of the late Mr Joseph Jones, Castle Bank, whose death we chronicled last week, took place on Saturday, in the presence of a large number of people. The chief mourners were Mrs Jones (widow), Misses Louie and Florrie Jones (daughters), Mrs Rowlands (sister-in-law), Mr Jones (brother), and the Rev J. R. Williams (cousin). A number of deceased's commercial friends acted as pall-bearers.

WHO?

Who is regarded by competent judges as one of the ablest members of the late Parliament?
MR LLOYD-GEORGE.

Who, according to John Burns, rendered Welsh miners and railwaymen signal service?
MR LLOYD-GEORGE.

Who is the member that would, according to Mr Perks, be greatly missed by English Nonconformists, if he were not re-elected?
MR LLOYD-GEORGE.

Who exposed the Kynoch scandal?
MR LLOYD-GEORGE.

Who protested against paying to British soldiers only a quarter of the wage paid to the Colonial?

Who induced the House of Commons to pass a resolution in favour of paying compensation to the widows of soldiers killed in war?
MR LLOYD-GEORGE.

Who has at all times pleaded for the rights of Wales and Welshmen?
MR LLOYD-GEORGE.

Who pointed out that the Chamberlain family firm prohibited trades unionism?
MR LLOYD-GEORGE.

Who fought for fair railway rates on the Chester and Holyhead line?
MR LLOYD-GEORGE.

Who has pleaded for progress and fairplay to Nonconformists in elementary and secondary schools?
MR LLOYD-GEORGE.

Who protested against taxing the country to support London parks and police courts?
MR LLOYD-GEORGE.

Who protested against the iniquity of taxing the towns for the benefit of agricultural landlords?
MR LLOYD-GEORGE.

Who saved £20,000 to the ratepayers of Carnarvon?
MR LLOYD-GEORGE.

Who did his utmost to help Conway to retain the headquarters of the police?
MR LLOYD-GEORGE.

Who helped Pwllheli to get a harbour of refuge constructed?
MR LLOYD-GEORGE.

Who powerfully helped to get Nevin a light railway?
MR LLOYD-GEORGE.

Who has served his constituency in every possible way, so as to deserve the best thanks and unabated confidence of the voters?
MR LLOYD-GEORGE.

CHEAP PRINTING at the "Herald" Office.

---

the deer to be paid in full at the rate of 10s a month.

CLAIM FOR CARTAGE.—Richard Edwards, carter, Croeswaen, Waen, sued Hughes, builder, of the same place, for balance due for cartage.—Mr R. peared for plaintiff, and Mr J. defendant.—It appears that the from the defendant insisting on cartage of timber by the ton and alleged by plaintiff was arrang was given for plaintiff for £4 1s 6

DE WINTON & CO.—was an action brought by Messrs Co., ironfounders, Kitchen, Drwsycoed, Trefriw, alleged due on extras made.—Mr peared for plaintiffs, and Mr W. P. Roberts Llanrwst, for defendant.—It appeared defendant was supplied by plaintiffs with a new boiler for his yacht, the contract for supplying which was £75. However, extras were ordered to be made outside that contract, and it was on account of those that the claim was made.—Mr W. P. Roberts contended that the amount paid under the contract included the extras now charged for.—His Honour asked for the contract, but as it was not forthcoming, owing to a technical point, the case was withdrawn, no costs being allowed.

CLAIM FOR GOODS.—Richard Hughes, grocer, Clynnog, sued Mrs Humphreys, Cae'rpwsan, of the same place, for £6 15s 6d, value of goods supplied. There was a counter-claim for £1 12s 6d.—Mr Richard Roberts appeared for plaintiff, and Mr Nath Roberts for defendant.—Judgment for plaintiff less counter-claim, to be paid at 10s a month.

CLAIM FOR DAMAGE.—J. Beynon Davies. fellmonger, Carnarvon, claimed £14 from the London and North-Western Railway Company for loss sustained by the defendants not delivering skins within reasonable time at Manchester, and skins lost in transit.—Mr R. Roberts appeared for plaintiff, and Mr Fenna represented the railway company.—Mr Fenna admitted the claim, but said that the consignment note which plaintiff had filled up withdrew all responsibility off the company's shoulders, as they were carried under special rates, and at owner's own risk.—Judgment for defendants with costs.

CLAIM FOR MEAT.—Messrs D. Evans and Co., butchers, Carnarvon, sued E. Pierce Jones, butcher, Talysarn, for £3 5s 2½d for meat supplied in 1895.—Mr Henwood appeared for defendant, and said his client denied that he owed a farthing to Mr Evans.—Mr R. Roberts, for the plaintiff, said the sum in dispute had been wrongly entered in another butcher's account by plaintiff's little boy, but after some time the mistake was found, and on turning to the daybook it was found that the amount now claimed was due from E. P. Jones.—His Honour suggested that as there was no certainty on the matter, they should split the amount, the parties agreed, and judgment entered for plaintiffs for that amount.

The question Synod comment include sixteen more than twice that number of adherents, shall be divided into two district of about equal size.

---

kindly undertaken the training of the pupil-teachers, and really splendid work had been done. She would be very sorry to have these replied any arrangements for changing classes, as it was not considered that the work interfered with the County School work.—Mr Jones Morris said that it would be fairer for the elementary school authorities at Penygroes to send their pupil-teachers to the intermediate school in the ordinary way.—Mrs W. A. Darbishire asked that permission be granted to go on as before until Christmas.—Mr Issard Davies agreed to this, and the request was granted. — Subject to this, the resolution was carried.

THE MANUAL INSTRUCTOR'S REPORT. —Mr John Evans's report was submitted. It announced that all the students who sat for examination in manual training of the City and Guilds of London had passed. Below is a list of the candidates:—John B. S. Cussons, County School, Portmadoc; Evan E. Davies, Board School, Llanberis; Edward Hughes, County School, Carnarvon; J. G. Jones, British School, Llanllechid; Wm. Meiwyn Jones, Board School, Talysarn; William Ll. Roberts, National School, Portdinorwic; Thomas Roberts, Board School, Glanweddyn, Conway; William Williams, County School, Llanrwst; Morris Williams, Board School, Carnarvon; William J. Williams, Board School, Llanberis; Lewis Ll. Williams, Higher Grade School, Blaenau Festiniog.

APPLICATIONS. — An application received from the Bangor (Friars School) Local Governing Body, for a special grant towards the expense of providing tools, &c., for manual instruction, was complied with.—An application from the Conway-Llandudno Loyal Governing Body for a grant to enable them to furnish a room for manual instruction, at an estimated cost of about £25, was also granted.

OLD

Many or disused turned in Fraser since 1833 your teeth turn past they will teeth or sary, app Inswich

Lloyd George, no doubt,
When his life ebbs out,
   Will ride on a flaming chariot,
Seated in state on red-hot plate
   'Twixt Satan and Judas Iscariot,
Ananias that day to the Devil will say,
   "My claim for precedence fails.
So move me up higher, away from the fire,
   And make way for the liar
   – from Wales".

Cân draddodiadol
Traditional song

'How can I convey to the reader who does not know him any just impression of this extraordinary figure of our time, this syren, this goat-footed bard, this half-human visitor to our age from the hag ridden magic and enchanted woods of Celtic antiquity.'

J M Keynes (1919)

"When I come along and say, 'Here, gentlemen, you have escaped long enough, it is your turn now. I want you to pay just 5 per cent on the £10,000 odd', they reply: '5 per cent? You are a thief; you are worse, you are an attorney; worst of all, you are a Welshman'. That always is the crowning epithet. I do not apologise, and I do not mind telling you that if I could I would not. I am proud of the little land among the hills, but there is one thing I should like to say – whenever they hurl my nationality at my head I say to them, 'You Unionists, hypocrites, Pharisees, you are the people who in every peroration always talk about our being one kith and kin throughout the Empire, from the old man of Hoy in the north down to Van Dieman's Land in the south, and yet if any man dares to aspire to any position, if he does not belong to the particular nationality which they have dignified by choosing their parents from, they have no use for him'. Well, they have got to stand the Welshman this time".

Lloyd George, October 1909

'Pe clywsai fy nhad i sicrwydd fod Mr Lloyd George wedi lladd ei nain, buasai mwrdro neiniau ar unwaith yn llai o ysgelerder yn ei olwg. Canys Mr Lloyd George oedd Pab Rhyddfrydiaeth; ac y mae popeth a wna'r Pab yn gyfreithlon ac yntau ei hunan yn anffaeledig. . .'

W J Gruffydd, 'Hen Atgofion'(1936)

'Lloyd George was from first to last a politician. He breathed politics every moment of the day. He believed that it was ultimately through political work that this world with all its injustices and cruelties, could be transformed and made more bearable for ordinary people.'

K O Morgan, 'D Lloyd George' (1981)

'Count up all his faults, set against them what he achieved, and it is difficult to resist the feeling that Lloyd George was the greatest ruler of England since Oliver Cromwell.'

A J P Taylor, rhagymadrodd i 'Lloyd George', K O Morgan (1974)

A J P Taylor's introduction to 'Lloyd George', K O Morgan (1974)

Bywyd Cynnar

Early Life

Yn 1858, penodwyd William George, Trecoed, Sir Benfro, mab i ffarmwr tenant, yn ysgolfeistr Ysgol Troedyrallt, Pwllheli. Yn Fedyddiwr ac o dan ddylanwad sosialaeth gydweithredol Robert Owen, cyfarfu yn 1859 ag Elizabeth Lloyd, a oedd yn gweini ym Mhwllheli, a'i phriodi y flwyddyn honno. Roedd hi'n ferch i Rebecca a Dafydd Llwyd, crydd pentref yn Highgate, Llanystumdwy. Yn 1861, cychwynnodd William George ar swydd ddysgu newydd ym Manceinion. Yno, yn 1863, y ganwyd David Lloyd George.

Yn fuan wedyn, gwaethygodd iechyd William a rhaid oedd iddo ddychwelyd i Sir Benfro i ffermio. Fodd bynnag, bu farw cyn bo hir, a dychwelodd ei weddw ifanc i Lanystumdwy i fyw yn Highgate gyda'i brawd Richard Lloyd, a oedd bellach yn gyfrifol am fusnes y crydd. Daeth y crydd patriarchaidd hwn o Fedyddiwr Albanaidd yn ddylanwad hollbwysig ar y Lloyd George ifanc.

Yn 1871, dim ond 76 teulu oedd yn byw ym mhentref plentyndod Lloyd George. Roedd mwyafrif y pentrefwyr yn labrwyr tlawd. Er bod Richard Lloyd yn gymharol lewyrchus, roedd bywyd y teulu ymhell o fod yn gyfforddus. Gadawodd y tlodi truenus yn y pentref, a dylanwad trwm y tirfeddiannwr Torïaidd Anglicanaidd lleol Ellis-Nanney o Blas Gwynfryn dros y plwyfolion, a oedd yn bennaf yn

In 1858, William George, of Trecoed, Pembrokeshire, the son of a tenant farmer, was appointed master of Troedyrallt School, Pwllheli. A Baptist influenced by the co-operative socialism of Robert Owen, in 1859 he met and married Elizabeth Lloyd, who was in domestic service at Pwllheli. She was the daughter of Rebecca and Dafydd Llwyd; her father was a village shoemaker at Highgate, Llanystumdwy. In 1861 William George took up a new schoolteaching post at Manchester. There, in 1863, David Lloyd George was born.

Shortly afterwards, William's health deteriorated. He had to return to Pembrokeshire to farm. He died soon after, however, and his young widow returned to Llanystumdwy to live at Highgate with her brother Richard Lloyd, who was now responsible for the shoemaking business. The patriarchical Campbellite Baptist pastor and shoemaker became the dominant influence on the young Lloyd George.

In 1871, Lloyd George's boyhood village consisted of a mere 76 households. Most of the villagers were poor labourers. Richard Lloyd was relatively prosperous, but life for the family was far from comfortable. The abject poverty in the village and the domination of the local Tory Anglican squire, Ellis-Nanney of Plas Gwynfryn, over a predominantly Nonconformist population

1. Richard Lloyd, ewythr Lloyd George, yng Ngharth Celyn, Criccieth, tua diwedd ei fywyd.

2. Elizabeth George, mam David Lloyd George.

3. William George, tad David Lloyd George.

4. Man geni Lloyd George, 5 New York Place, Chorlton-upon-Medlock, Manceinion.

1. Richard Lloyd, Lloyd George's uncle, at Garth Celyn, Criccieth, towards the end of his life.

2. Elizabeth George, David Lloyd George's mother.

3. William George, David Lloyd George's father.

4. Lloyd George's birthplace 5 New York Place, Chorlton-upon-Medlock, Manchester.

Anghydffurwyr, argraff annileadwy ar Lloyd George. Yn nes ymlaen, dywedodd mai Llanystumdwy oedd "Y Plwyf Torïaidd duaf yn y wlad".

Yn yr ysgol Eglwys Seisnig leol, disgleiriodd yn ei waith, ond gwrthryfelodd yn erbyn ei dylanwad Anglicanaidd. Yn 1878 ymadawodd â'r ysgol i fwrw'i brentisiaeth fel twrnai gyda Breese Jones a Casson, ym mhorthladd llechi llewyrchus Porthmadog. Ar ôl ei gymhwyso ei hun yn 1884, sefydlodd ei fusnes ei hun yng nghartref newydd ei ewythr, Morvin House, yng Nghricieth, ac ym Mhorthmadog. 'Roedd, felly, ar drothwy gyrfa wleidyddol egniol fel radical Anghydffurfiol a chenedlaetholwr ymosodol.

5

made an indelible impression on Lloyd George, leading him later to name Llanystumdwy as 'the blackest Tory Parish in the land'.

At the local Anglicised Church school he excelled at his work but rebelled against its Anglican influence. In 1878 he left school to be articled as an attorney with Breese, Jones and Casson in the flourishing slate port of Porthmadog. After qualifying in 1884, he set up in business on his own at his uncle's new home, Morvin House, Criccieth and at Porthmadog. Thus, he was poised to enter upon an active and scintillating career as a thrusting Nonconformist, Liberal-nationalist politician.

6

5. Crydd a gyflogwyd gan Richard Lloyd, y tu allan i'r gweithdy yn Highgate, Llanystumdwy, oddeutu 1870.

6. Lloyd George yn fachgen ifanc 16 mlwydd oed.

7. Highgate, cartref ei blentyndod.

8. Plas Gwynfryn, cartref sgweiar pentref Llanystumdwy, H J Ellis-Nanney.

9. Yr Hen Efail, Llanystumdwy, 'Senedd y Pentref'.

5. A cobbler employed by Richard Lloyd outside the workshop at Highgate, Llanystumdwy, circa 1870.

6. Lloyd George as a youth of sixteen.

7. Highgate, his boyhood home.

8. Plas Gwynfryn, the Llanystumdwy home of the village squire, H J Ellis-Nanney.

9. The Old Smithy, Llanystumdwy, the 'Village Parliament.'

"My supreme idea is to get on. To this idea I shall sacrifice everything — except I trust honesty. I am prepared to thrust even love itself under the wheels of my juggernaut."

Lloyd George at Margaret Owen   Lloyd George to Margaret Owen

Y Gwleidydd a'r AS Ifanc

Fel cyfreithiwr ifanc gyda diddordeb brwd mewn gwleidyddiaeth, defnyddiodd Lloyd George y llysoedd i ennill enwogrwydd fel amddiffynwr y gwan. Gwnaeth 'Twrnai'r Potsiars' ei argraff ddyfnaf yn ystod Achos Claddu Llanfrothen, 1888, pryd y daeth yn enwog drwy Gymru gyfan, am amddiffyn yn athrylithgar, hawl chwarelwr tlawd i gladdedigaeth Anghydffurfiol ym mynwent y plwyf.

Hefyd, yn 1888, sefydlodd ei bapur newydd cyntaf, *Udgorn Rhyddid*, ym Mhwllheli, a daeth yn flaenllaw iawn mewn cylchoedd Rhyddfrydol lleol gyda'i weithgareddau yn 'Rhyfel y Degwm' ac fel arweinydd lleol y Cynghrair Tirol, Masnachol a Llafurol Gymreig. Erbyn 1889, roedd wedi sicrhau enwebiad seneddol etholaeth Bwrdeisdrefi Caernarfon, er gwaethaf gelyniaeth Rhyddfrydwyr cymedrol, ac yn yr un cyfnod, ychwanegodd at ei fri drwy gael ei benodi i wasanaethu ar Gyngor cyntaf Sir Gaernarfon fel y 'Bachgen Henadur'.

Erbyn 1890 roedd yn Aelod Seneddol ar ôl cael buddugoliaeth gofiadwy mewn is-etholiad annisgwyl ym Mwrdeisdrefi Caernarfon a sicrhaodd gyhoeddusrwydd enfawr iddo. Gorchfygodd 'mab y bwthyn' ei sgweiar Torïaidd lleol, H J Ellis-Nanney, o 18 pleidlais yn unig, ar ôl ail-gyfrif dadleuol.

Yn fuan iawn, gwnaeth argraff fawr yn San Steffan fel pencampwr disglair materion Cymreig a beirniad tanbaid Rhyddfrydiaeth Gladstonaidd. Fel arweinydd Cynghrair Cymru Fydd, daeth i wrthdrawiad chwyrn â'i Blaid ei hun, a bu hyn yn un o'r rhesymau dros gwymp y Llywodraeth Ryddfrydol yn 1895. Serch hynny, parhaodd i ymgrychu dros Ymreolaeth i Gymru hyd nes i'r mudiad ddarfod yn 1896. Wedyn er iddo barhau i ymddiddori mewn materion Cymreig, treuliodd ei amser fwyfwy gydag achosion gwleidyddol Prydeinig.

The Young Politician and MP

As a young solicitor, passionately interested in politics, Lloyd George used the courts to gain renown as a radical Liberal and a champion of the underdog. The 'Poacher's Advocate' made his greatest impact during the Llanfrothen Burial Case of 1888, when his brilliant defence of a poor quarryman's right to a Nonconformist burial in the parish churchyard brought him recognition throughout Wales.

In 1888, too, he founded his first newspaper, *Udgorn Rhyddid* (The Trumpet of Freedom) at Pwllheli, and his involvement in the Tithe War as a local leader of the Welsh Land, Commercial and Labour League brought him to considerable prominence in local Liberal circles. By 1889 he had secured the Liberal parliamentary nomination of the Caernarfon Boroughs constituency despite the hostility of moderate Liberals. In the same period, he added to his prestige by being appointed to serve on the first ever Caernarvonshire County Council as 'the Boy Alderman'.

By 1890 he was an MP having secured a notable victory at an unexpected, highly publicised by-election in the Caernarfon Boroughs, when the 'Cottage-bred boy' defeated his local Tory Squire H J Ellis-Nanney by the tiny margin of eighteen votes, after a controversial recount.

He soon made his mark at Westminster, emerging as a flamboyant champion of Welsh affairs and an outspoken critic of Gladstonian Liberalism. This brought him through his leadership of the Cymru Fydd (Young Wales) League, into bitter confrontation with his own Party. This contributed to the downfall of the Liberal Government in 1895. Nevertheless, he continued to champion the Welsh Home Rule issue until the movement's demise in 1896. Thereafter, though retaining an interest in Welsh affairs, he devoted himself increasingly to general British political causes.

10. Lloyd George, yr AS ifanc.   **10.** Lloyd George, the young MP.

11

13

13

THE HERALD

THE BURIAL SCANDAL AT LLANFROTHEN.

THE CASE BEFORE THE PORTMADOC COUNTY COURT.

VERDICT FOR THE DEFENDANTS.

THE Rev. Richard Jones, rector of Llanfrothen, Dean Lewis, of Bangor, and Archdeacon Evans of Llanllechid, sued Mr. Morris Roberts, Gareg, Llanfrothen, and seven others at the Portmadoc County Court, on Wednesday, for damages, the allegation being that defendants had unlawfully broken into part of the burial ground attached to the church at Llanfrothen, and of which the plaintiffs alleged they were trustees. Our readers will remember that when the funeral of the late Mr. R. Roberts, Chapel House, Croesor, arrived at the entrance to the churchyard, they found the gate locked ; and as the friends of the deceased had given notice to the rector that the funeral would take place under the Burials Act, believing that they had a legal title to the burial ground, they forced open the gate and buried deceased in a grave which had once been closed at the request of the rector. Naturally, the case created profound interest in the neighbourhood, and the court was densely packed throughout the hearing of the case by Judge Bishop and the following gentlemen as a jury:—Mr. E. M. Roberts (Ffriddfedw, Talsarnau), Capt. Morgan Jones, Messrs. John Owen (Paris House), Morris E. Morris (chemist), and Robert Owen (timber merchant); Messrs. Lloyd Carter and Vincent, Carnarvon, appeared for plaintiffs, and Mr. D. Lloyd George and Mr. W. George, Criccieth, for defendants and for the vestry of Llanfrothen parish. The case having been opened by Mr. Carter, the following

12

11. Cartŵn politicaidd, 1892.

12. Adroddiad o'r *Carnarvon and Denbigh Herald*, 18 Mai 1888, ar y gwrandawiad cyntaf o 'Achos Claddu Llanfrothen'.

13. Giât mynwent y plwyf, Llanfrothen, y cynghorodd y cyfreithiwr ifanc, Lloyd George, deulu Robert Roberts i'w datgloi er mwyn sicrhau cynhebrwng teilwng i'r chwarelwr Anghydffurfiol, 1888.

14. Menter newyddiadurol gyntaf Lloyd George, *Udgorn Rhyddid*, a gyhoeddwyd gyntaf ym Mhwllheli, Ionawr 1888. Mae'r rhifyn hwn, 19 Rhagfyr 1888, yn cynnwys adroddiad ar ddiweddglo llwyddiannus i Achos Claddu Llanfrothen.

11. A political cartoon, 1892.

12. A report in the *Carnarvon and Denbigh Herald*, 1 May 1888, of the first hearing of the 'Llanfrothen Burial Scandal' case.

13. The gate to the Parish Churchyard at Llanfrothen which Lloyd George, the young country attorney, advised Robert Roberts's family to break open to proceed with the poor Nonconformist quarryman's funeral in 1888.

14. Lloyd George's first newspaper venture, *Udgorn Rhyddid* (The Trumpet of Freedom) first published at Pwllheli, January 1888. This edition, of 19 December 1888, includes an article reporting the successful outcome of the Llanfrothen burial case.

UDGORN RHYDDID.

(The Trumpet of Freedom)

Newyddiadur Cenedlaethol Cymreig.

| RHIF 51. CYF. II. | DYDD MERCHER, RHAGFYR 19, 1888. | (REGISTERED FOR TRANSMISSION ABROAD.). Pris Dimai· |

Y Prif Gwnstabl a Helynt y Degwm yn Llannor.

PAN ar fyned i'r wasg cawsom ar ddeall fod y Prif Gwnstabl wedi anfon llythyr at y Parch. D. E. Davies, yn datgan ei ddiolchgarwch gwresocaf iddo am gydsynio a'i gais trwy fyned i Lannor dydd Gwener diweddaf, ac am ei ymdrech ef ac eraill o arweinwyr y bobl i gadw trefn. Teimlwn yn ddiolchgar i Col. Ruck am ei foneddigeiddrwydd yn cydnabod hyn. Efallai y cawn y llythyr i'w gyhoeddr eto.

Derbyniasom y llythyr canlynol oddiwrth Mr. Carter, fel copi o'r hyn a anfonwyd at 7 rhai yr ntafaelwyd eu heiddo, 'a cofyn arnom ei gyhoeddi yn yr UDGORN :—

Rhag. 17eg, 1888.

Anwyl Syr,—Dymunaf gyflwyno fy niolchgarwch diffuant i chwi a phlwyfolion eraill am eich hynaswsdd i mi dydd Gwener diweddaf, tra yr oeddwn yn ceisio cyflawni dyledswydd tra anymunol. Pa wahanol olygiadau bynag a ddigwyddwn goleddu, gallwn oll gyd-lawenhau yn y ffaith y medr cynifer o'n cyd-wladwyr ymgynull ynghyd heb droseddu y gyfraith.

Yr eiddoch yn gywir,

H. LLOYD CARTER.

ACHOS CLADDU LLANFROTHEN.

BUDDUGOLIAETH ARDDERCHOG.

Bydd cofus gan ein darllenwyr am yr achos pwysig hwn, yn mha un yr hawlnu Rheithor Llanfrothen gan allan ran o fynwent y plwyf oddiwrth y plwyfolion. Daeth yr achos ymlaen yn y Llys Sirol yn Mhorthmadog, pryd y barnodd y rheithwyr mai i'r plwyf yr ydoedd y darn tir dan sylw wedi ei roddi fel cyhwarogfa i'r fynwent. Ond rhoddodd y Barnwr Bishop ei ddedfryd yn erbyn y plwyfolion serch hyny. Apeliodd y plwyfolion i'r Uchel Lys yn Lundain, a dydd Sadwrn a Llun diweddaf daeth yr achos ymlaen. Ymddangosai Mr. Bompas, Q.C., a Mr. T. E. Scrutton, (yn cael eu cyfarwyddo gan Mri. Lloyd George & George, Criccieth), dros y plwyfolion, a Mri Jeune, Q.C., a J. E. Vincent (yn cael eu cyfarwyddo gan Mri. Lloyd Carter & Vincent, Carnarvon), dros y Rheithor. Yr ydym newydd dderbyn y newydd boddhaol fod y plwyfolion wedi cario'r dydd, a bod y barnwr wedi uchel gondemnio ymddygiad y Clerigwr a Barnwr y Llys Sirol yn y mater. Ceir manylion pellach y tro nesaf.

Yr Anrhydeddus Frederick Wynn a'i Denantiaid.

Yr ydym yn deall fod Mr. Wynn wedi cyfarwyddo ei oruchwyliwr, Mr. Richard Roberts, i ganiatau rhodd yn ol 10 y cant i'r holl denantiaid amaethyddol ar ei ystad yn Sir Gaernarfon a Sir Fôn, a fyddant wedi talu eu degwm hyd Gorphenaf diweddaf.

MARWOLAETH MR. ROBERT OWEN, PWLLHELI.

Boreu Mercher diweddaf brawychwyd trigolion Pwllheli a'r amgylchoedd a'r newydd galarus o farwolaeth un o'n trefwyr mwyr parchus, sef Mr Robert Owen, Llyfrwerthydd. 'Roedd yn un o'n masnachwyr mwyaf cyfrifol ac yn gristion a berchid gan bawb yn gyffredinol. Cymerodd ei anghladd i dydd Llun, pryd y talodd cannoedd o bobl eu teyrnged olaf o barch iddo.

CYNGHOR SIROL
SIR GAERNARFON.

At Etholwyr Sirol
Dosbarth Llanengan a Llangian.

Foneddigesau a Boneddigion.

Wedi ymgyndynu mor hir yn erbyn ceisiadau fy nghyfeillion, gwel pawb o honoch mai nid awydd am anrhydedd personol sydd yn fy nghymell i ddyfod allan yn ymgeisydd i'ch cynrychioli ar y Bwrdd Sirol. Wrth gael llais clir a diamwys fy nghyd-drethdalwyr fel ei ddadganwyd yn y cyfarfod a gynhaliwyd yn Llanengan, nos Sadwrn y 24ain, o'r mis hwn, y penderfynais gymeryd y cam presenol. Gwyr pawb beth yw fy syniadau, ac hefyd nad oes dim wedi arfer fy lluddiais i weithredu yn ol fy marn. Fel y gweithredais yn y gorphenol, y bydd i mi wneud eto yn y dyfodol. Os etholir fi ni fydd dim a'm rhwystra i wneud fy ngoreu er amddiffyn buddianau ffermwyr a gweithwyr y wlad, yn mysg pa rai yr wyf yn awr yn cartrefu ers blynyddau, ac wedi dyfod i wybod am eu hanawderau a'u hangenhion. Anfonaf ddatganiad llawn o'm hegwyddorion i bob etholwr yn ystod yr wythnos hon.

Meddaf yr anrhydedd o fod

Eich ufudd was

ABEL WILLIAMS,

Tach 26ain, 1888. Abersoch.

Y CYNGOR SIROL.

AT ETHOLWYR LLEYN AC EIFIONYDD.

Anwyl Gydwladwyr,

Yr ydym ni sydd a'n henwau isod, ymgeiswyr am aelodaeth ar y Cynghor Sirol dros wahanol Ranbarthau yn Lleyn ac Eifionydd, trwy hyuywa yn dymuno datgan ein golygiadau ar y materion Sirol a drosglwyddir dan Gyfraith y Llywodraeth Leol i ofal y Cynghorau hyn :—

1. Yr ydym yn ffafriol i'r Gymraeg fod yn Iaith Llafar yn eisteddiadau y Cynghor.

2. Hyd y byddo yn bosibl, yr ydym yn ffafriol i benodiad Cymry yn Swyddogion dan y Cynghor.

3. Yr ydym yn erbyn cyflogau gormodol a phob gwastraff afreidiol; ac yr ydym o'r farn y dylai y cyflogau a delir o'r Dreth Sirol gael eu penodi gan y Cynghor.

4. Yr ydym o blaid gweinyddiad Cyfraith Cadwraeth yr Afonydd i fod mor ffafriol ag sydd bodd er mantais y Werin.

5. Yr ydym yn bleidiol i ddiwygiad yn nghyfundrefn yr Heddlu, ac yn credu y dylent fod yn gyfangwbl o dan reolaeth y Cynghor; a bod profiad a theilyngdod yn amod dyrchafiad i'r swyddau uchaf.

7. Ymdrechwn ymgyrhaedd at gyfoedeb ac effeithiolrwydd yng(lyn â chadwraeth y Ffyrdd a'r Pontydd.

8. Eiu bod yn hysfyried yn bwysig i gael dynion Ryddfrydig i wir gynrychioli syniadau y wlad tuag at iddynt roddi eu llais o blaid neu yn erbyn mesurau a gynygir yn y Senedd Ymherodrol.

9. Yr ystyriwn yn bwysig cael dynion all gydymdeimlo a masnachwyr a ffermwyr y wlad i gyfarfod a Dirprwywyr y Rheilffordd, er cael ffraul cludiad nwyddau mor isel ag sydd fodd.

Meddwn, yr anrhydedd o fod,

Foneddigesau a Boneddigion,

Eich Ufudd Wasanaethyddion,

JOHN T. JONES, Criccieth.
WM. ROBERTS, Moelfre fawr.
J. H. DAVIES, Caertyddyn.
H. TUDWAL DAVIES, Bryullaeth.
ABEL WILLIAMS, Abersoch.
O. W. GRIFFITH, Mela.
WM. WILLIAMS, Pwllerwn.

CYNGHOR SIROL
SIR GAERNARFON.

AT ETHOL WYR NEFYN, CEIDIO, A BODFEAN.

Foneddigesau a Boneddigion.

Ar ddymuniad nifer luosog o Etholwyr y rhanbarth uchod, ac hefyd fel dewisedig y blaid Ryddfrydol a gynhaliwyd yn Nefyn Nos Sa' n diweddaf, dymunaf gynyg fy hun am yr a rhydedd o'ch cynrychioli yn y Cynghor Sirol.

Gan fy mod yn adnabyddus i chwi o'm mebyd, hyderaf nad rhaid i mi wrth lythyrau canmoliaeth.

Y mae fy ngolygiadau gwleidyddol hef-yd mor hysbys i chwi fel nad wyf yn tybied fod angen am f mi ond yn unig eich sicrhau y bydd fy ymlyniad yn egwyddorion mawrion Rhyddfrydiaeth mor gadarn a diysgog yn y dyfodol ag y bu yn y gorphenol, a chaiff rhaglen awdurdodedig Cynghor Cenedlaethol Cymreig fy nghefnogaeth wresocaf a mwyaf calonog.

Nid ydyw cri y Toriaid nad oes gwleidyddiaeth (politics) ar eth presenol ond ystwr er enill ple Na thwyller chwi. Rhyddf Theriaeth sydd yn y glorian, cyfrifoldeb o droi y fanto mewn rhan arnoch chwi, Eth Ceidio, a Bodvean.

Hyderaf y bydd i chw gwaho ddiad gwresog ro ldar allan fel ymgeisydd. drwy cynrychiolydd ddydd yr ' drechaf Sheu sich awai lawn ar bob pwnc a all go Sirol, leol, yn cystal a ch

Gan fy mo l yn bwriadu gyfarfodydd yn y gwahan datgan yn mhellach fy n perthynas a'r pwnc gwir b eraf y gwnewch bob ymdre presenoldeb yn y cyfryw.

Yr eiddoch, Foneddigesau a yn ostyngedig,

Mela, O. W. Gl Rhag. 10, 1888.

Eisteddfod Gadeiriol Gwyn

CYNHELIR CYNGHERDD yn y N Drefol, Pwllheli, nos Iau, Ionawr 1889, yn yr hwn y bydd cystadle mewn canu unrhyw Solo, y gynulleidfa n blaen-seddau i feirniadu.

14

Liberal candidate.

THE POLLING DAY.

The polling took place on Thursday. The population of the boroughs, according to the census of 1881, was 28,391, and the present electorate numbers 4628, distributed as follows:—Carnarvon, 1517; Bangor, 1509; Conway, 580; Pwllheli, 522; Nevin, 370; and Criccieth, 215. The following are the results of previous elections:—

1885.

Mr. Jones Parry (L.)	...	1923
Mr. Swetenham (C.)	...	1858
Majority	...	65

1886.

Mr. Swetenham (C.)	...	1820
Mr. Jones Parry (L.)	...	1684
Majority	...	136

CARNARVON.

Polling began very briskly at the two booths in Carnarvon, no fewer than 50 electors recording their votes during the first half-hour, both parties being well represented.—In the Western Ward polling booth (Guild Hall), Mr. Richard Parry acted as presiding officer; Mr. E. H. Morris being the polling clerk. Mr. W. J. Williams was in charge of the Liberal committee rooms, while Mr. George Owen took charge of the Conservative committee rooms, assisted by Mr. J. M. Clayton. The first that voted was Mr. Robert Roberts, tailor, Northgate-street. Up to one o'clock about 400 persons had voted, which number was increased by 7 p.m. to 720. The presiding officer at the Eastern Ward (the polling station for which was the National School) was Mr. R. Ll. Jones, Mr. William Evans acting as the polling clerk. The Liberals were represented by Messrs. John Jones, druggist, and R. O. Roberts, solicitor, while the Conservatives were represented by Mr. John Williams, saddler. Mr. J. T. Parry took charge of the Liberal committee rooms, and Mr. H. Ll. Carter of the Conservative committee rooms, assisted by Mr. J. J. Roberts. The first to record his vote was Mr. J. Owen Jones, Eryri Shop, Pool-street. Up to 12 noon about 300 had voted, and by 5 p.m. the number had increased to 500. Both parties were well supplied with vehicles, those on the Liberal side being lent by Mrs. Pugh, Llysmeirion; Colonel Hunter, Plas Coch, Anglesey; Mr. Owen Jones, Green Bank; Mr. J. Thomas, broker; Mr. Jones Hughes, Post-office, Rhostryfan; Mr. O. Jones, Bronceres; Mr. Walker Hughes, Penrhos; Mr. Edward Hughes, ironmonger; Mr. Herbert Jones, Penygroes; Mr.

all was creating immense interest in the hearts of the people.

RESULT.

The result of the election was declared by the Mayor as follows:—

Lloyd-George	...	1963
Ellis-Nanney	...	1945
Majority	...	18

THE VICTORIOUS CANDIDATE.

Mr. Lloyd George was drawn in a carriage through the town by tremendous crowd, and he was accompanied by Mr. Acland, M.P., Mr. John Bryn Roberts, M.P., Dr. E. O. Price, Bangor, Mr. J. T. Roberts, and others. Arriving at Castle-square, Mr. Lloyd George, speaking in Welsh, but first of all greeted with "three cheers for the boy M.P.," which were lustily given, said:—My dear fellow-countrymen, the county of Carnarvon to-day is free (loud cheers). The banner of Wales is borne aloft and the boroughs have wiped away the stains (loud cheers). I hope that whoever will be contesting the next election (cries "It will be you") will not fail to achieve a similar victory. The contest has been carried on by both sides in the best possible good humour. It has been a battle of principle (cries, "Coal," and laughter). I thank you from my heart, and all those who have worked so hard for the Liberal cause. I specially wish to thank the Ladies' Liberal League (three cheers were here given to the Ladies' League). Mr. George concluded by saying that he hoped the majority would be largely increased by the general election.

The carriage afterwards proceeded up Pool-street, followed by a great crowd.

After the declaration of the poll, Mr. Ellis Nanney was carried to the Conservative Club by his supporters with almost as much shouting as if he had been victorious. The large room of the club was at once filled with a large and excited crowd, who, for about five minutes, cheered Mr. Ellis Nanney in a remarkably lusty fashion. The cheers having subsided, Mr. Ellis Nanney rose and addressed his supporters. He said he was very happy to meet them all at the close of the contest which had been so gloriously fought, and which he regretted to say they had not won ("Shame"). The

ly, the defendant himself in the sum of £10, an one surety in the sum of £20.

Home Rule all Round.

RADICAL LEADERS SNUB THE IDEA.

In the current issue of "Young Wales," the main feature is an article by Mr Lloyd George, M.P., on "National Self-Government for Wales," and a discussion under the heading, "Our Round Table Conference," in which, in reply to an invitation from the editor, a certain number of leading Radicals express their views on "Home Rule all Round" in preference to disestablishment as the foremost plank. Altogether there are no less than 22 who have a word to say on the question. Mr Gladstone comes first, but he refuses to say "yes" or "no," being afraid that any opinion from him would "be more likely to cause embarrassment than advantage." Mr Asquith declares that "the matter is not one in which he has any title to intervene." Sir H. H. Fowler "is not prepared to express an opinion." Sir Robert T. Reid, after a dig at the House of Lords and a snub to Welsh Disestablishers, pooh-poohs the Home Rule all round fad. Sir Frank Lockwood laughs at the idea, and closes with fine ridicule. "I have not read the Home Rule All Round Bill nor have I met with anyone who has." Sir Walter Foster wisely asks, "How can Home Rule all round, or even disestablishment, be carried under the supremacy of the House of Lords?" Mr Justin M'Carthy disclaims his ability to utter an opinion—a thing he evidently has not got on the question. Mr R. B. Haldane, Q.C., promises "to watch with interest the progress of the movement." Sir George Osborne Morgan prefers riding his old hack, Welsh Disestablishment, deeming it unwise to swop horses in crossing the stream. Mr T. P. O'Connor advises "Young Wales" to read some "lucid" speeches of his, and speaks of Home Rule for Ireland. Mr Timothy Healy is "not in a position to enter into the question." Sir Edward Grey does not think himself "competent, nor has he any desire, to give any advice upon a question of tactics." Mr D. A. Thomas rides behind Sir George Osborne Morgan on the old Disestablishment back. Mr R. W. Perks considers the Young Wales Party as "demented" destroyed, in fact, by the gods. Mr John Dillon thinks it is a question for Welsh Liberals, the while keeping his eye on Irish Home Rule. Mr John Redmond is "most strongly opposed" for substituting "Home Rule all round" for "Home Rule for Ireland." Mr Henry Broadhurst agrees with the scheme, but regrets that Disestablishment "is not making great progress." Mr Joseph Arch swallows the pills, box and all. Mr R. M'Kenna, before replying, must feel the pulse of his "constituents." Mr Clifford Cory does not think Home Rule for Wales is "generally asked for." Mr Owen Phillips, Liberal candidate for the Montgomery Boroughs, jumps at the bait dangled before him. The Rev. Hugh Price Hughes, who comes in at the tail, puts on shoulder a plea for Home Rule and the other under Welsh Disestablishment.

Thus "Young Wales" has received but little encouragement from the first meeting of its "Round Table Conference" to proceed with "Home Rule all Round."

15. Canlyniad is-etholiad 1890 ac adroddiad ar ddigwyddiadau terfynol yr ymgyrch, *Carnarvon and Denbigh Herald*, 11 Ebrill 1890.

16. Adroddiad o'r newyddiadur Toriaidd, *The North Wales Chronicle*, 26 Hydref 1895, a adlewyrcha y gwrthwynebiad Rhyddfrydol i arweiniad Lloyd George o'r ymgyrch Senedd Gartrefol i Gymru.

17. Llun etholiadol Lloyd George pan ddychwelwyd ef am y tro cyntaf fel AS Bwrdeisdrefi Arfon, 1890.

15. The by-election result 1890, and an account of the closing stages of the campaign, *Carnarvon and Denbigh Herald*, 11 April 1890.

16. A report from the Bangor Tory newspaper, *The North Wales Chronicle*, 26 October 1895, revealing the Liberal opposition to Lloyd George's championing of the Home Rule for Wales campaign.

17. Lloyd George's election photo taken when he was returned for the first time as MP for the Caernarfon Boroughs, 1890.

16 Municipal Nominations.

LLOYD GEORGE ESQ MP
...RED DISGUISED AS A LOYAL SUBJECT.
...RMINGHAM DEC 1...1901

"The money that would have built comfortable homes for hundreds of thousands of our fellow men has gone to dig graves in South Africa." Lloyd George 1900

Dod i Amlygrwydd Prydeinig, 1899-1905

Yr hyn a ddaeth â Lloyd George i sylw cyhoeddus eang ym Mhrydain oedd ei amddiffyniad tanbaid, ac yn aml amhoblogaidd, o achos y Boeriaid yn ystod Rhyfel y Boer. Siaradodd mewn cyfarfodydd stwrllyd ledled Prydain, yn cynnwys un yn ei etholaeth ei hun ym Mangor pryd yr ymosodwyd arno gan dorf anystywallt. Pan alwyd yr 'Etholiad Khaki' yn 1900 gan y Llywodraeth Doriaidd i sicrhau cefnogaeth i'w safiad gwrth-Boeraidd, ymladdodd Lloyd George ymgyrch feiddgar yn ei etholaeth ei hun, gan ennill buddugoliaeth ryfeddol, er gwaetha'r ymosodiadau chwyrn a wnaed arno oherwydd iddo gefnogi'r Boeriaid. Wedi'r etholiad, parhaodd â'i ymgyrch ddigyfaddawd, gan ymestyn y frwydr, hyd yn oed i gadarnle Torîaidd, gwrth-Foeraidd Chamberlain, yn Birmingham, lle y llwyddodd i ddianc o grafangau torf ffyrnig, wedi ei wisgo fel plismon.

Wedi'r rhyfel, bu yng nghanol berw gwleidyddol arall fel arweinydd y 'Gwrthryfel Cymreig' yn erbyn Deddf Addysg Balfour, 1902, pan geisiodd y Llywodraeth Dorîaidd orfodi'r Awdurdodau Addysg i roi arian o'r trethi i gynnal ysgolion eglwysig, cais a wrthwynebid yn chwyrn gan yr Anghydffurfwyr Cymreig. Fel arweinydd y gwrthwynebiad i'r Ddeddf, daeth Lloyd George yn gocyn hitio'r cartŵnwyr yn y Wasg Dorïaidd. Fodd bynnag, parodd Diwygiad Crefyddol 1904-05 ragor o elyniaeth i'r Ddeddf yng Nghymru. Gyda chymorth pregethwyr grymus y Diwygiad, megis y Parch Evan Roberts, parhaodd yr ymgyrch drefnus a llwyddiannus hyd dymchweliad y Llywodraeth Dorîaidd yn 1905. Wedyn, fel aelod o'r Cabinet yn y Llywodraeth Ryddfrydol newydd, defnyddiodd ei ddylanwad i sefydlu Adran Gymreig y Bwrdd Addysg, a ystyrid yn fuddugoliaeth i anghydffurfiaeth yng Nghymru.

Emerging to British Prominence, 1899-1905

The one issue which brought Lloyd George widespread public attention in Britain was his militant and often unpopular advocacy of the Boers' cause during the Boer War. He addressed rowdy meetings throughout Britain, including one in his own constituency at Bangor where he was attacked by a mob. When the Tory government called the 'Khaki Election' of 1900 to secure support for its anti-Boer stance, Lloyd George fought a daring campaign in his own constituency and won a remarkable victory despite violent attacks upon him for his pro-Boer views. After the election he continued his uncompromising campaign, carrying the battle even into the Tory anti-Boer stronghold of Chamberlain's Birmingham, where he escaped from a ferocious mob disguised as a policeman.

After the war he again became the centre of controversy when he led the 'Welsh Revolt' against Balfour's Education Act of 1902, by which the Tory government compelled Local Education Authorities to make money from the rates available to church schools, a move deeply resented by Welsh Nonconformists. As leader of this opposition to the Act, Lloyd George became the victim of catoonists in the Tory press. However, hostility to the Act in Wales was heightened by the Religious Revival of 1904-05. With the aid of powerful Revivalist preachers, such as the Revd. Evan Roberts, the well orchestrated successful campaign continued until the downfall of the Tory Government in 1905. Then, as a member of the Cabinet in the new Liberal Government he used his influence to secure a Welsh Department of the Board of Education, which was regarded as a victory for Nonconformity in Wales.

18. Cerdyn Post poblogaidd sy'n darlunio dihangfa Lloyd George, wedi ei wisgo fel heddwas, o grafangau torf enfawr pro-Boeraidd yn Neuadd y Dref, Birmingham, 18 Rhagfyr 1901.

18. A popular postcard depicting Lloyd George's escape from the Town Hall, Birmingham, disguised as a policeman, following a pro-Boer riot, 18 December 1901.

THE CARNARVON BOROUGHS.

REMARKABLE VICTORY.

ENTHUSIASTIC SCENES.

CARNARVON, SATURDAY NIGHT.

I am but a Saxon, and words fail me to describe the scenes of delirious enthusiasm which I have just witnessed in this little borough of Carnarvon. The welcome of a people to their triumphant champion, the expression of a great relief, the reaction from a great fear. For when, after a long day of working and suspense, the figures revealed an increase of over 100 on the previous poll, then came recoil from dread to exultant triumph. Great joy sometimes kills, and the delirium of the people became a positive peril to their hero, who was almost sacrificed to the frenzied worship of his followers. Never do I remember such a scene of ecstasy. It had been a long, anxious day for all the Liberals in the boroughs, who had alternate fits of hope and fear, sanguine assurance and perilous despondency. These feelings varied very much with the districts; for while in Bangor and Carnarvon the Liberals were perhaps too anxious, the little townships of Criccieth, Nevin, and Pwllheli already simmered with satisfaction. "Wales expects Nevin to do its duty" wired Mr. Lloyd-George at midday, finding himself unable to get as far as the remote little township, which lies on the northern coast of the peninsula and faces the Atlantic with an open courage that should breed the finest politicians. Nevin stoutly replied, and from Pwllheli came the same note of cheerful confidence. More than half the town had polled before midday. When we arrived at Criccieth in the afternoon every face was wreathed with smiles—"All polled but fifty, and they sure." But Bangor openly gave warning of an increased majority against us, and the Carnarvon people shook their heads. It all seemed to depend on which was stronger—the eastern boroughs or the western. Such are the doubts and anxieties of a fight which extends over six small townships, perhaps the most difficult electoral battle that any man can wage.

But now work was over, and the issue lay within the Carnarvon Town Hall, whither the ballot-boxes have been brought by the evening trains to be counted the same evening. And then great throngs of people began to come from the neighbouring districts into Carnarvon. Processions began to parade the streets, singing election songs and shouting for their favourite candidate. There was no mistake as to the voice of these crowds. In the afternoon I had seen some flag-waving processions, especially one of boys escorting the embarrassed Colonel Platt,

could reach, wild with excitement and expectation. From the crowd came a combat of songs—first from one side "Rule Britannia," then from the other that great Welsh anthem "Land of Our Fathers," swelling up in greater and greater volume until the song of menace and aggression was drowned in the song of freedom and home-love as the Venus music in the "Tannhäuser" is drowned in the Pilgrims' March. Then as the time went on rumours began to ooze from the counting-room, as they always will ooze, in spite of all regulations of concealment—first "George in," then "George in by 300," then "George in by 200," then "George in between 200 and 300." The rumours flew up and down the town, invading whole streets, setting processions moving, adding van loads and windows full of citizens to the loud-voiced triumph. But the more prudent held back, waiting for the official figures.

It was close upon midnight when the suspense ended, and the Mayor stepped out on the balcony of the Town Hall. "Lloyd-George," he cried, but he could say no more. One mighty shout rose from the multitude beneath. No future word could be heard. Then came delirium. It began with the usual appearance on the balcony, but it did not reach fever pitch until Mr. Lloyd-George, finding that no carriage came through the crowd, essayed to reach the Liberal Club under the escort of six constables. He might just as well have relied on a set of corks to face the rapids of Niagara. The love of those people was almost terrible; it was certainly dangerous. They closed upon their hero, they wrung his hand till it almost came off, they patted his back until it almost broke, they drowned his protests in their shouts. Manfully the constables fought their way forward, but from above Mr. George's white hat looked like a little paper boat in a raging sea. And so they brought him to the door of the club, a helpless hero, a conqueror almost slain by his own conquest. We well knew how dangerous these jokes may be. Mr. Cowen was once nearly killed thus. And so there we closed round him and carried him up the stairs through the throngs on to the balcony outside. Mr. William Jones, M.P., who has played a yeoman's part in this contest, at last obtained silence, and then Mr. Lloyd-George spoke a few of those brief, pregnant sentences which he knows well how to coin. "While England and Scotland are drunk with blood, the brain of Wales remains clear, and she advances with steady step on the road of progress and liberty." A mighty shout rose up, such as rose when, in 1895, he cried from the same window that the wave of reaction had broken on the rocks of Snowdon. Then occurred the noblest scene of all. Descending from the balcony, we mounted into a brake, where Mr. Lloyd-George could be seen of all and yet saved from their too perilous attentions. This brake was filled with the untiring lieutenants who have brought Mr. Lloyd-George safely through the fight. They advanced slowly down the main street, the crowd with one consent formed up behind in marching column, and as they marched they sang. Ah! how these Welshmen sang the old election song of the Carnarvon boroughs:—

Hurrah! hurrah! We're ready for the fray.
Hurrah! hurrah! We'll drive Sir John away.
The grand young man will triumph; Lloyd-George
 will win the day.
Fight for the freedom of Cambria.

They sang it to "Marching through Georgia," the song to which a continent has fought two wars and will yet fight another. It is one of the best marching songs in the world, and looking back on that great multitude you saw its tread become perfectly rhythmic; its confusion become order; delirium pass under the magic of a song, the mob became an army. And so they marched through the whole town, while every window and doorstep was filled with waving hats and handkerchiefs. It was like the welcome of a king returning from his wars. The darkness seemed to matter nothing, all seemed lightness to-night. The enemy, so strong at midday, had disappeared. Seized by a sudden inspiration, Mr. Lloyd-George stood upright in the carriage, and so with lifted hat met the multitudes face to face with a happy smile. A few months ago they had stoned him, a few weeks ago they were still against him; but now with silver tongue he had won back their hearts, and his people were with him again. Surely, few men have ever tasted such an hour. The procession reached the end of its journey. Then Mr. George called for silence and asked them to sing once more "Land of Our Fathers." In a moment there was utter stillness, and then they sang that great and solemn anthem. The darkness above us lent the scene a ghostly majesty; the earnest, melancholy harmonies breathed an undying hope; the sea of invincible faces gave a sense of vast, indefinable strength. The great hymn ended, and then in perfect quiet the great multitude dispersed. And so was a victory for courage and principle which in this election will hold a historic place second to no other.

HAROLD SPENDER.

Majority		61

1895—L U, 5,990; L, 5,921. Liberal Unionist majority, 78.

CARNARVON DISTRICT.

D. Lloyd-George (L)	2,412
Colonel Platt (C)	2,116
Majority	296

1895—L, 2,265; C, 2,071. Liberal majority, 194.

FLINT DISTRICT.

J. H. Lewis (L)	1,760

20

19. Adroddiad o'r *Manchester Guardian*, 8 Mawrth 1900, gan Harold Spender sy'n disgrifio'r adwaith frwdfrydig yng Nghaernarfon i fuddugoliaeth Lloyd George ym Mwrdeisdrefi Arfon yn yr 'Etholiad Khaki', 1900.

20. Canlyniad etholiad 1900 ym Mwrdeisdrefi Arfon.

21. Adroddiad o Derfysg Birmingham, 18 Rhagfyr 1901 o'r *Illustrated London News*, 28 Rhagfyr 1901.

22. Sgets o Derfysg Birmingham o'r *Illustrated London News*, 28 Rhagfyr 1901.

parting passengers is brought to the vans

THE BIRMINGHAM RIOT.

On the evening of Dec. 18, when Mr. Lloyd-George came to Birmingham to address a meeting in the Town Hall, under the auspices of the Liberal Association, certain supporters of the Government created a serious obstruction. Early in the day it had become known that opposition might be expected, for the tickets had been forged, and this necessitated the issue of others bearing the secretary's signature. The precaution, however, was in vain, and from the hour of assembling it was evident that many enemies were in the hall. When the organist struck up "Men of Harlech," the tune was greeted with a storm of booing and hissing; and when Mr. Lloyd-George came on the platform he was not allowed a hearing. It is understood that he said : " This is rather lively for a peace-meeting," and for a time he gallantly strove to address the reporters. Matters, however, became very serious. The reporters' platform was carried by the rioters, and but for the sturdy efforts of a strong body of police, the speakers themselves would have been rushed. For a while they stood their ground, but at length when stones and pen-knives, accompanied by copper coin (these last probably to prevent the cutting of friendship), began to come through the windows, Mr. Lloyd-George was persuaded to retire. He ultimately made his escape from the hall in a police-inspector's uniform, and it is said that he marched out in line with a dozen officers. Outside in the streets there was severe fighting, and one youth was killed.

21

22

. A report from *The Manchester Guardian*, 8 October 1900, by Harold Spender, describing the enthusiastic response at Caernarfon to Lloyd George's victory in the Caernarfon Boroughs 'Khaki Election', 1900.

. The result of the election of 1900 in the Caernarfon Boroughs.

. A report of the Birmingham Riot of 18 December 1901 from *The Illustrated London News*, 28 December 1901.

. A sketch of the Birmingham Riot from *The Illustrated London News*, 28 December, 1901.

23

23. Lloyd George a'r Pregethwr Diwygiad enwog, y Parch Evan Roberts yn teithio i gyfarfod yn Llandrindod Wells yn ystod y 'Diwygiad Mawr' 1904-05.

24. Cartŵn o'r *Western Mail*, 11 Gorffennaf 1902, yn beirniadu Lloyd George arweinydd y 'Gwrthryfel Cymreig' yn erbyn yr Ysgolion Eglwysig.

25. Cartŵn arall o eiddo'r *Western Mail*, 6 Hydref 1902, sy'n beirniadu Lloyd George a'r 'Gwrthryfel Cymreig'.

23. Lloyd George and the notable Welsh Revivalist preacher, the Reverend Evan Roberts, travelling to a meeting at Llandrindod Wells during the period of the 'Great Revival' 1904-05.

24. A cartoon from *The Western Mail*, 11 July 1902, criticising Lloyd George's leadership of 'The Welsh Revolt' against the Church Schools.

25. Another *Western Mail* cartoon (6 October 1904) criticising his involvement in the 'Welsh Revolt'.

24

A Prophet of Evil.

"Onward Christian Soldiers."

COMMANDANT LLOYD-GEORGE: Forward, my men; be brave and fear not! It will be the school children who will suffer—not us.

26. Portread o Lloyd George yn ystod
helyntion 'Cyllideb y Bobl' 1909.

26. A portrait of Lloyd George during the
controversy over the 'People's Budget' 1909.

Y Diwygiwr Cymdeithasol, 1906-1914

Swydd Gabinet gyntaf Lloyd George oedd fel Llywydd y Bwrdd Masnach, pryd y cyflwynodd fesurau fel y Ddeddf Llongau Masnach, a sicrhai amodau gwaith boddhaol i forwyr, mater o ddiddordeb iddo ers ei ddyddiau cynnar ym Mhorthmadog. Gyda'i benodiad yn Ganghellor y Trysorlys yng Nghabinet Asquith yn 1908 arloesodd raglen o ddiwygiadau cymdeithasol. Yn gyntaf, darparwyd Pensiwn i'r Henoed a gydnabyddid yng Nghymru fel 'Coron Lloyd George', sef y 5 swllt yr wythnos a delid i bensiynwyr sengl. Yn ei enwog 'Gyllideb y Bobl' (1909), 'i ymladd brwydr ddigyfaddawd yn erbyn tlodi a budreddi' trethodd y cyfoethog er lles yr anfreintiedig. Adlewyrchai hyn ei awydd angerddol, ers yn ifanc, i weld cyfiawnder cymdeithasol, awydd a feithrinodd Yncl Lloyd 'gwir awdur y gyllideb'. Cafwyd ymateb chwyrn i'r gyllideb. Gwrthodwyd hi gan Dŷ'r Arglwyddi yn Nhachwedd 1909 a gorfu i'r Llywodraeth alw Etholiad Cyffredinol yn Ionawr 1910. Denodd yr etholiad sylw rhyngwladol. Ymgyrchodd Lloyd George yn frwd yn ystod yr etholiad a bu rhaid iddo, ar adegau, osgoi helynt mewn rhai ardaloedd gelyniaethus. Ar ôl yr etholiad daeth ei gyllideb yn gyfraith gwlad yn Ebrill 1910. Wedi hynny, 'roedd yn benderfynol o danseilio grym yr Arglwyddi. Bu'n amlwg yn yr etholiad a alwyd ym mis Rhagfyr i ennill cefnogaeth gyhoeddus i gyfyngu ar rym yr Arglwyddi. Enillodd y Rhyddfrydwyr ac, yn 1911, pasiwyd Deddf y Senedd a rwystrai'r Arglwyddi rhag atal deddfwriaeth ariannol a basiwyd eisoes gan Dŷ'r Cyffredin; hefyd, lleihawyd dylanwad yr Arglwyddi dros fesurau eraill. Yna, aeth Lloyd George ymlaen i'w gamp fawr nesaf, sef Deddf Yswiriant Gwladol 1911, uchafbwynt ei raglen ddiwygiadol a sicrhaodd iddo enwogrwydd fel 'Sylfaenydd y Wladwriaeth Les'. Parhaodd i gefnogi achosion Anghydffurfiol Cymreig ei yrfa gynnar gan annerch cyfarfodydd mawr ar Ddatgysylltiad yr Eglwys yng Nghymru yn ei etholaeth. Fodd bynnag, ni phlesiai'r 'Suffragettes' fel diwygiwr cymdeithasol a tharfwyd ar ei gyfarfodydd yn fynych.

The Social Reformer, 1906-1914

Lloyd George's first Cabinet post was as President of the Board of Trade, when he introduced measures such as the Merchant Shipping Act, which prescribed decent working conditions for sailors, a matter of concern to him since his early days at Porthmadog. With his appointment as Chancellor of the Exchequer in Asquith's Cabinet, in 1908, he embarked on a programme of social reform, the first stage of which was the provision of Old Age Pensions, the 5s a week paid to single pensioners being known in Wales as 'Coron Lloyd George'. His famous 'People's Budget', introduced in 1909 'to wage implacable warfare against poverty and squalidness', taxed the wealthy to provide for the under-privileged. This reflected his passionate concern since childhood for social justice, nurtured in him by Uncle Lloyd – 'the real author of the budget'.

It was rejected by the House of Lords in November 1909 forcing the government to call a General Election in January 1910. The election attracted international attention and Lloyd George campaigned vigorously, having to take evasive avion in some hostile areas. After the election his budget became law in April 1910. He was then intent upon undermining the power of the Lords. In the election called in December to win public support to limit the power of the Lords, Lloyd George played a prominent role. The Liberals won, and in 1911 passed the Parliament Act, which prevented the Lords from vetoing finance legislation approved by the Commons, and reduced their influence over other measures. Lloyd George then went on to his next great achievement, the National Insurance Act of 1911. This was the culmination of his reform programme, which established his reputation as the 'Founder of the Welfare State'. He also found time to pay lip service to the Welsh Nonconformist reforms of his early career, addressing large Welsh Church Disestablishment meetings in his constituency. His reputation as a social reformer was not held in high esteem by the suffragettes who continually attacked his approach to Women's Suffrage.

28

THE PHILANTHROPIC HIGHWAYMAN.
Mr. Lloyd George. "*I'll make 'em pity the aged poor!*"

[August 5, 1908.]

29

30

27. Lloyd George gyda'i ferch hynaf, Mair Eluned, a fu farw yn ddwy ar bymtheg mlwydd oed yn 1907. Bu ei marwolaeth yn gyfrwng iddo gysegru ei hun i'w raglen o ddiwygiadau cymdeithasol wedi 1908.

28. Lloyd George yn ei swydd Lywodraethol gyntaf, Llywydd y Bwrdd Masnach 1906-08.

29. Cartŵn *Punch*, 5 Awst 1908, sy'n dangos y cythrwfwl a fu ynglŷn â Deddf Pensiynau i'r Henoed, 1908.

30. Thomas Thomas, y gof o Wyddelwern, Meirionnydd, y pensiynwr cyntaf yng Nghymru i dderbyn y pensiwn, pum swllt yr wythnos – 'Coron Lloyd George'.

27. Lloyd George with his eldest daughter, Mair Eluned, who died at the age of seventeen in 1907. Her death impelled him to immerse himself in his programme of social reform after 1908.

28. Lloyd George's first Government post as President of the Board of Trade 1906-08.

29. A *Punch* cartoon, 5 August 1908, depicting the controversy which arose over the Old Age Pensions Act of 1908.

30. Thomas Thomas, blacksmith of Gwyddelwern, Merioneth, the first pensioner in Wales to receive Lloyd George's five shillings per week – 'Coron Lloyd George'.

31

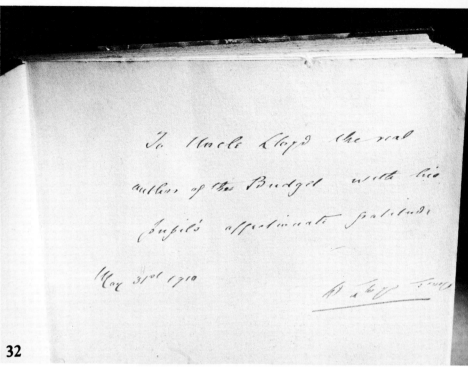

32

31. Lloyd George, Canghellor y Trysorlys, gydag Uncle Lloyd yn 11 Stryd Downing yn ystod cyfnod 'Cyllideb y Bobl'.

32. Cydnabyddiaeth o ddiolchgarwch Lloyd George i Richard Lloyd wedi ei ysgrifennu y tu mewn i glawr copi cyntaf o'r Ddeddf a ymgorfforai ddiwygiadau 'Cyllideb y Bobl'.

33. Lloyd George, yn 45 mlwydd oed, yn fuan wedi ei benodi'n Ganghellor y Trysorlys, 1908, gydag argymhellion ei Gyllideb yn gefndir priodol.

31. Lloyd George, the Chancellor of the Exchequer, with Uncle Lloyd at 11 Downing Street, during the period of the 'People's Budget'.

32. Lloyd George's gesture of acknowledgement to Richard Lloyd, written on the flyleaf of the Act, when the 'People's Budget' became law in May 1910.

33. Lloyd George at 45 years of age, the newly appointed Chancellor of the Exchequer, 1908, with his Budget proposals as an appropriate backcloth.

RICH FARE.

The Giant Lloyd-Gorgibuster: "FEE, FI, FO, FAT,
I SMELL THE BLOOD OF A PLUTOCRAT;
BE HE ALIVE OR BE HE DEAD,
I'LL GRIND HIS BONES TO MAKE MY BREAD."

Bernard Partridge.

34. Cartŵn *Punch*, 28 Ebrill 1909 yn portreadu Lloyd George fel yr 'Anghenfil' yng ngolwg yr aristocratiaid a'r cyfoethogion.

35. Adwaith y Wasg i benderfyniad Tŷ'r Arglwyddi wrthod 'Cyllideb y Bobl', 1 Rhagfyr 1909.

36. Megan Lloyd George, yn blentyn, yn canfasio etholwyr yng Nghaernarfon gyda chynrychiolydd etholiadol ei thad, Nath Roberts, yn ystod Etholiad Ionawr 1910 a alwyd i gadarnhau cefnogaeth y cyhoedd i 'Gyllideb y Bobl'.

37. Lloyd George yn annerch cyfarfod ar y Maes, yng Nghaernarfon, yn ystod un o Etholiadau Cyffredinol 1910. Galwyd yr ail etholiad (Rhagfyr) sicrhau cefnogaeth i gyfyngu pwerau Tŷ'r Arglwyddi.

38. Cerdyn Post a gyhoeddwyd yn 1911 sy'n dathlu Deddf Yswiriant Genedlaethol 1911, Lloyd George

34

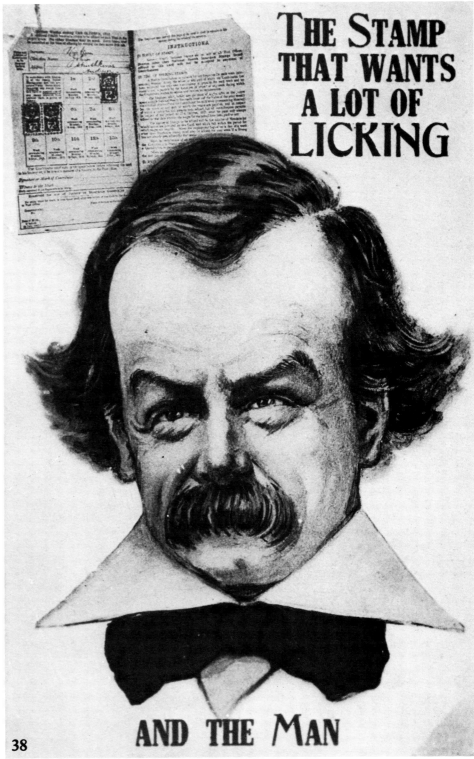

THE STAMP
THAT WANTS
A LOT OF
LICKING

AND THE MAN

36. A *Punch* cartoon, 28 April 1909. portraying
Lloyd George as the 'Ogre' feared by the aristocracy
and the wealthy.

37. The response of the Press to the House of Lords'
rejection of the 'People's Budget', 1 December 1909.

38. The young Megan Lloyd George canvassing at
Caernarfon with Nath Roberts, her father's election
agent, during the January election of 1910, called to
confirm public support for the 'People's Budget'.

39. Lloyd George addressing an election meeting at
Castle Square, Caernarfon during one of the two
General Elections of 1910. The second (December)
election was called to secure support for limiting the
powers of the House of Lords.

40. Picture postcard published in 1911, celebrating
Lloyd George's National Insurance Act 1911.

38

THE CHANCELLOR TICKLED!

THE CHANCELLOR QUELLING THE

. Lloyd George yn annerch cyfarfod enfawr i hybu hos Datgysylltu'r Eglwys Anglicanaidd yng ghymru, yn y Pafiliwn, Caernarfon, 1912.

. Cyfarfod arall Datgysylltu'r Eglwys yn y filiwn ar drothwy'r Rhyfel Mawr.

. Ellis Jones Griffith, AS Rhyddfrydol Sir Fôn, yn nerch cyfarfod dathlu agoriad Neuadd y Pentref, anystumdwy, ym Medi 1912, anrheg gan Lloyd orge i'r plwyf.

. Yn yr un cyfarfod, tarfwyd ar araith Lloyd orge gan nifer o 'suffragettes', a brotestiai yn byn ei wrthwynebiad i fudiad Mrs Pankhurst, ndeb Cymdeithasol a Pholiticaidd y Merched.

39. Lloyd George addressing a huge Welsh Church Disestablishment meeting at the Caernarfon Pavilion, 1912.

40. Another Church Disestablishment meeting at the Pavilion on the eve of the Great War.

41. Ellis Jones Griffith, Liberal MP for Anglesey, speaking at the meeting in September 1912, to celebrate the opening of the Llanystumdwy Village Institute, donated to the parish by Lloyd George.

42. At the same meeting, Lloyd George's speech was interrupted by several suffragettes, who disliked his opposition to Mrs Pankhurst's Women's Social and Political Union.

"We had to join the struggle or stand aside and see Europe go under and brute force triumph over public right and international justice." Lloyd George 1918

Arweinydd mewn Rhyfel a Heddwch, 1914-1922

1914 oedd y flwyddyn y dechreuodd y Rhyfel Mawr yn erbyn yr Almaen. Er bod gan Lloyd George amheuon ynglŷn â'r rhyfel, ar y cychwyn, buan y sylweddolwyd y byddai'n rhaid ymdrechu i'r eithaf i sicrhau buddugoliaeth i'r Cynghreiriaid. Pan oedd achos y Cynghreiriaid ar ei wannaf, fe'i apwyntiwyd i'r Weinyddiaeth Arfau newydd yn 1915, a thra yno llywddodd i adfywio'r ymgyrch ryfel gan sefydlu ei hun fel y ffigwr mwyaf deinamig yn y Llywodraeth Glymbleidiol. Ym Mehefin 1916 penodwyd ef yn Ysgrifennydd Gwladol Rhyfel, ac ym mis Rhagfyr, yn dilyn beirniadaeth gynyddol ar arweinyddiaeth Asquith, fe'i dewiswyd yn Brif Weinidog fel y 'dyn i ennill y Rhyfel'. Fel Prif Weinidog, defnyddiodd ei benderfyniad di-ildio a'i ddoniau areithio, perswadio, a threfnu, yn ogystal â'i allu strategol treiddgar i arwain Prydain a'r Cynghreiriaid i fuddugoliaeth erbyn 1918.

Yn adnabyddus drwy'r byd fel un o brif benseiri'r fuddugoliaeth, 'roedd Lloyd George, fel arweinydd etholedig y Llywodraeth Glymbleidiol newydd, i chwarae rhan holl bwysig yng Nghynhadledd Heddwch Versailles. Ond er gwaethaf ei ymdrechion glew i sicrhau cytundeb cymhedrol a pharhaol bu'r cytundebau a wnaed yn gyfrwng i hau gwrthdaro yn y dyfodol yn Ewrob a esgorodd ar yr Ail Ryfel Byd.

Yn y cyfamser, fe wynebai broblem ddyrys Iwerddon, ail-adeiladu'r economi ac aflonyddwch diwydiannol. Fel arweinydd clymblaid anesmwyth gyda'r Torîaid cododd wrychyn y mudiad llafur yn arbennig, oherwydd iddo fethu gwladoli'r pyllau glo, fel yr argymhellodd Comisiwn Sankey yn 1919, ac hefyd oherwydd anallu'r llywodraeth i ddelio â'r dirwasgiad economaidd yn 1920. 'Roedd wedi methu gwneud y wlad yn 'Land fit for heroes to live in'. Erbyn 1922, fe'i gwnaed yn fwch-dihangol gan y Torîaid oherwydd amhoblogrwydd y Glymblaid, ac fe'i gorfodwyd i roi'r gorau i'w swydd. Ni chafodd, byth wedyn, flasu'r grym mawr a brofodd fel arweinydd mewn rhyfel a heddwch.

43. Lloyd George, Prif Weinidog y Glymblaid, 1920.

The Leader in War and Peace, 1914-1922

1914 saw the outbreak of the Great War against Germany. Although Lloyd George initially had reservations about the war, he came to realise that only a supreme effort would secure victory for the Allies. When he was appointed to the newly created Ministry of Munitions in 1915, with the Allied cause at its lowest ebb, he regenerated the war effort and emerged as the most dynamic figure in the Coalition government. In June 1916 he became Secretary of State for War and in December, following mounting criticism of Prime Minister Asquith's leadership, he was chosen to replace him as 'the man to win the war'. As Prime Minister he used his ruthless determination and gifts of oratory, persuasion, organising ability, and imaginative strategic thinking to lead Britain and her Allies to victory by 1918.

Acclaimed throughout the world as one of the main architects of victory, Lloyd George, now elected as leader of the new post-war Coalition government, played a dominant role at the Versailles Peace Conference. But, despite his valiant attempts to obtain a moderate and durable settlement, the treaties which followed were to sow the seeds of future conflict in Europe, culminating in the Second World War.

Meanwhile, at home, he faced the daunting problems of Ireland, economic reconstruction and industrial unrest. As leader of an uneasy coalition with the Tories, he antagonised the labour movement particularly by his failure to nationalise the coal mines, as had been advocated by the Sankey Commission of 1919, and by his government's inability to deal with the economic recession of 1920. He had failed to build 'a land fit for heroes to live in'. By 1922, the Tories were prepared to make him a scapegoat for the Coalition's unpopularity, and he was forced to leave office, never again to exercise the supreme power he had held as leader in war and peace.

43. Lloyd George, the Prime Minister of the Coalition Government, 1920.

LLOYD GEORGE SHELLS.

An officer of the Durhams, who took part in the battle of Hooge, has written to a friend at Hitchin, describing the final charge, and adds:—

"It was the new Lloyd George shells which gave us the heart to make the charge, after being so heavily hit. These new shells are magnificent an after our fellows got into the captured trenches they gave three cheers for Lloyd George."

46

44. Lloyd George, y Gweinidog Arfau, yn arolygu'r 'Home Guard' ym Mangor, 1915.

45. Gweithwyr arfau, gan gynnwys 'munitionettes' o Gaernarfon, 1915.

46. Adroddiad o'r *Carnarvon and Denbigh Herald*, 27 Awst 1915, yn clodfori gwaith Lloyd George fel Gweinidog Arfau.

47. Milwyr y tu allan i Orsaf Reilffordd, Caernarfon yn 1915, ar eu ffordd i Gallipoli.

48. Milwyr Cymreig o ardal Caernarfon 'rhywle yn Ffrainc' 1915.

49. Lloyd George a'i gyfaill mynwesol, Winston Churchill yn cyd-gerdded yn Whitehall, 1915.

44. Lloyd George, Minister of Munitions, inspecting the Home Guard at Bangor, 1915.

45. Munitions workers, including 'munitionettes' from Caernarfon, 1915.

46. Report from the *Carnarvon and Denbigh Herald*, 27 August 1915, praising Lloyd George's work as Minister of Munitions.

47. Recruits outside Caernarfon Railway Station, 1915, on their way to Gallipolli.

48. Welsh soldiers from the Caernarfon area 'somewhere in France' 1915.

49. Lloyd George and his great friend Winston Churchill strolling down Whitehall, 1915.

Mr. LLOYD GEORGE ON PATRIOTISM

THE RECORD OF WALES.

Speech at the Eisteddfod.

In accordance with his practice for some years, Mr Lloyd George attended the National Eisteddfod on Thursday at Bangor, and presided over the meeting, at which the ceremony of Chairing the Bard took place. The right hon. gentleman, accompanied by Mrs Lloyd George and Miss Megan Lloyd George, travelled specially from London, and upon his arrival received a great welcome from an audience numbering between 8000 and 10,000.

In the name of "ten thousand" Welshmen the meeting passed a resolution conveying an expression of unchangeable loyalty to the throne, and their unalterable constancy to the allied cause in these days of stress and strain.

Mr Lloyd George, who was received with prolonged cheers, accompanied by the playing of "For he's a jolly good fellow" by the Royal Marine Band, said:

Dear fellow-countrymen. However great a being a Welshman may be, he must have a day at the Eisteddfod. I am only a bit of a Welshman in an office in London—(laughter)—and I have escaped from it for one day of Welsh song, and since I came here I have done a little business. The first thing I had was a letter handed to me by the conductor of the Eisteddfod. I opened it, and found it to be a letter for a man who had been singing here and had not succeeded in the competition. Now he is asking me if there is a vacancy for him in the Munitions Office in London (loud laughter). And as there will be more losers than winners in the Eisteddfod I hope to go back to London with a good sized army of helpers to supply munitions of war for the Allies (laughter and cheers).

A NATIVE OF THE HILLS.

I have come here from the work of war in order to hear the harp of the bards above the shriek of the shell (cheers). I observe that you have omitted to ask the old Eisteddfod question, "Is it peace?" What is the good of asking it? Everywhere sounds of war; trumpets rend the air from sea to sea, the land of Britain trembles in the march of myriads preparing for war. East and west and north and south you hear the ring of the hammers and the whistle of the steel lathes fashioning weapons of war. On quiet nights from my cottage in Surrey I can hear the sound of the cannon fired in anger on the ruddier fields of death in France. I know with horror the work that is going on, and as I hear it the old prayer of the Gorsedd comes to my lips, "O Iesu nad Gamwaith" (Oh, Jesus, prevent the wrong) (hear, hear).

51

50. Adroddiad o araith 'Ddydd Iau' Lloyd George, y Gweinidog Arfau, oddi ar lwyfan Prifwyl Eisteddfod, Bangor 1915. *Carnarvon and Denbigh Herald*, 4 Awst 1915.

51. Lloyd George yn annerch torf enfawr o 10,000 yn Eisteddfod Genedlaethol Bangor, 1915.

52. Lloyd George y Gweinidog Rhyfel, yn cwrdd â Syr Douglas Haig, y Cadfridog Joffre a Monsieur Thomas (Gweinidog Arfau Ffrainc), ar y Ffrynt Gorllewinol, Medi 1916.

50. A report of Lloyd George's 'Thursday' speech, as Minister of Munitions, from the Eisteddfod platform at Bangor 1915. *Carnarvon and Denbigh Herald*, 4 August 1915.

51. Lloyd George addressing a mighty crowd of 10,000 at the Bangor National Eisteddfod of 1915.

52. Lloyd George, Minister of War, meets Sir Douglas Haig, General Joffre and Monsieur Thomas (French Minister of Munitions), on the Western Front, September 1916.

53

Lloyd George on the Western Front, September 16, with Monsieur Thomas.

The War Minister visits the trenches, September 16.

54

THE NEW CONDUCTOR.

OPENING OF THE 1917 OVERTURE.

56

55. *Punch*, Rhagfyr, 1916, yn darlunio Lloyd George yn meddiannu'r Brif Weinidogaeth.

56. Fel Prif Weinidog, cadwodd Lloyd George ei 'Gysylltiadau Cymreig' – darlun ohono yn 10 Stryd Downing gyda'r 'Cadfridog', y Parch John Williams, Brynsiencyn a'r athronydd Cymreig enwog, Syr Henry Jones, Llangernyw.

57. Y Prif Weinidog yn St Andrew's Hall, Glasgow Gorffennaf, 1917, yn galw am adfer annibyniaeth Serbia a Gwlad Belg ac yn cyhoeddi methiant ymgyrch llongau tanfor yr Almaen.

58. Y Prif Weinidog yn ymweld â ffatri awyrennau, 1917.

, Lloyd George's assumption of the Premiership
ptured by *Punch*, December 1916.

. As Prime Minister, Lloyd George maintained his
Velsh Connections' at 10 Downing Street –
otographed with 'General', the Rev John
illiams, Brynsiencyn and the noted Welsh
ilosopher, Sir Henry Jones, Llangernyw.

. The Prime Minister at St Andrew's Hall,
asgow, July 1917, calling for the restoration of
rbian and Belgian independence and announcing
e failure of the U-Boat campaign.

. The Prime Minister visiting an aeroplane
ctory, 1917.

59

60

59. Orlando (yr Eidal), Lloyd George, Clemenceau (Ffrainc) a Woodrow Wilson (UDA), yn y Gynhadledd Heddwch, yn Versailles.

60. Poblogrwydd Lloyd George, yr arweinydd rhyfel, wedi ei ddarlunio yn *Punch* ym 1919.

61. Lloyd George yn cefnogi 'Dydd y Pabi'.

. Orlando (Italy), Lloyd George, Clemenceau
rance) and Woodrow Wilson (USA), attending the
eace Conference at Versailles.

. Lloyd George's popularity as war leader
ptured by *Punch* in 1919.

. Lloyd George and the 'Poppy Day' Appeal.

61

62

64

63

65

62. Michael Collins, un o arweinyddion y ddirprwyaeth Wyddelig a lofnododd y Cytundeb sefydlodd y Wladwriaeth Rydd Wyddelig, yn 1921

63. Arthur Griffith, aelod arall o'r Ddirprwyaeth Wyddelig a fu'n flaenllaw yn y trafodaethau gyda Lloyd George a arweiniodd i lunio Cytundeb y Wladwriaeth Rydd Wyddelig.

64. Llofnodion Cytundeb y Wladwriaeth Rydd Wyddelig, 6 Rhagfyr 1921. Mae llofnod Lloyd George ar ben rhestr y llofnodwyr Prydeinig tra bo'r Gwyddelod wedi llofnodi eu henwau hwy yn y Wyddeleg.

65. Lloyd George yn mwynhau egwyl bwrw Sul yn rhydd o bryderon ei Brif Weinidogaeth olaf ac yn ymlacio ar yr aelwyd yn Llyfrgell Chequers, Mawrth 1922.

66. Lloyd George, gyda chlwb golff yn ei law, yn fuan wedi'r datganiad fod ei lywodraeth Glymblaid ar ben, Hydref 1922.

67. Ffarwel olaf Lloyd George â Stryd Downing wedi ei ddarlunio gan newyddiadur y cyfnod, *The Sphere*, 4 Tachwedd 1922.

2. Michael Collins, one of the leading members of the Irish delegation which eventually signed the agreement which established the Irish Free State in 1921.

3. Arthur Griffith, another member of the Irish delegation who negotiated with Lloyd George the Irish Free State Treaty.

4. The signatories to the Irish Free State Agreement, 6 December 1921. Lloyd George's signature leads the British signatories while the Irish signatories have all signed their names in Gaelic.

5. Lloyd George enjoying a weekend break from the toils of his Coalition premiership and relaxing by the fireside in the Library at Chequers in March 1922.

6. Lloyd George, with a golf club in his hand, after the announcement of the end of his Coalition government, October 1922.

7. Lloyd George's 'Good-bye to Downing Street', captured by a contemporary journal, *The Sphere*, 4 November 1922.

The Table at which Mr. Lloyd George Presided
The famous Cabinet room at No. 10

Two Interested Spectators of the Removal Operations at No. 10

Megan's last Public Appearance with her Father as Coalition Prime Minister

The Departure of Mr. Lloyd George, his Family, and Secretariat from No. 10

Mr. Lloyd George and his family left Downing Street last week for 86, Vincent Square, Westminster. The departure from office of a Prime Minister is always marked in this somewhat drastic manner, by an immediate vacating of No. 10. Furniture vans from various well-known firms rolled into the quiet little street, and into them went the personal belongings and furniture of the ex-Prime Minister. The family quietly took their departure for their new temporarily engaged home in Vincent Square. The Secretariat packed up their voluminous papers and left in their own way. The removal operations at one moment were watched by Sir Robert Horne and Sir L. Worthington-Evans, a little snapshot of whom appears on this page. Opposite appears a little group showing Miss Lloyd George or "Megan," as she was popularly known during her father's brilliant "Conference" period—at the opening of the new P.L.A. building. It was her last public appearance with her father during his term of office as Coalition Prime Minister. Dr. Macnamara also figures in the little group.

The quiet-looking portal, with its eighteenth-century fanlight above, has opened to many a strange and interesting gathering during Mr. Lloyd George's tenure of office. Stirring and even stormy scenes have been witnessed beneath the iron lamp with its little surmounting crown, and in the pillared chamber, designed by the architect, William Wilkins, who also did work in connection with Downing College, many an important meeting, conducted in the new manner, has taken place.

This famous house has been the residence of the First Lord of the Treasury, during his term of office, since 1735. The First Lord is, of course, nearly always the Prime Minister. The street was named after Sir George Downing, whose grandson founded Downing College. The first Prime Minister to reside in Downing Street was the famous Sir Robert Walpole. All his successors have followed this practice with the exception of Lord Melbourne, Sir Robert Peel, and Lord Salisbury. Next door to No. 10 lives the Chancellor of the Exchequer and at No. 12 is the office of the Government Whips. Nelson and Wellington once met at No. 14.

Mr. and Mrs. Lloyd George Leaving Downing Street Last Week

Mr. Lloyd George Superintending the Removal Operations at Downing Street

No. 18, Abingdon Street, which Mr. Lloyd George has Taken as Political Headquarters

Y Dewin yn y Cysgodion

The Wizard in the Wings

Rhwng y ddau ryfel byd, gorfodwyd Lloyd George, gwleidydd mwyaf deinamig y cyfnod, i sefyll o'r neilltu tra 'roedd dynion llai galluog yn ymrafael â phroblemau dirwasgiad, diweithdra ac anhrefn rhyngwladol. Yn anterth y dirwasgiad, cynigiodd 'Fargen Newydd', i'r di-waith, rhaglen feiddgar o fuddsoddi cyhoeddus a wrthodwyd gan bob llywodraeth yn ei thro. Er ei anwybyddu gan y gwleidyddion a feddai'r grym, parhaodd yn eilun i'r Cymry, gan lywyddu bob blwyddyn yn yr Eisteddfod Genedlaethol ar y dydd a gydnabyddid fel 'Diwrnod Lloyd George'. Yn y tridegau diweddar, fodd bynnag, ymneilltuodd fwyfwy o'r llwyfan gwleidyddol gan dreulio mwy a mwy o amser ar ei fferm yn Churt, Swydd Surrey.

Gyda'r bygythiad cynyddol i heddwch yn Ewrop trwy weithgareddau'r Almaen Natsiaidd ail-ymddangosodd i lansio ei ymgyrch olaf. Am gyfnod byr, roedd Lloyd George, cefnogwr pybyr yr Iddewon, wedi'i hudo gan lwyddiant Hitler wrth ail-adeiladu economi'r Almaen, ond buan yr argyhoeddwyd ef gan ddigwyddiadau diweddarach, a gyrhaeddodd ben llanw gydag argyfwng Munich, pa mor ffôl oedd polisi heddychiad Neville Chamberlain. Yn y ddadl allweddol bwysig yn Nhŷ'r Cyffredin, ar Fai 8fed 1940, cafwyd ymyriad grymus gan Lloyd George:

"I say solemnly that the Prime Minister should give an example of sacrifice, because there is nothing which can contribute more to victory in this war than that he should sacrifice the seals of office".

Ar 10 Mai, ymddiswyddodd Chamberlain ac fe'i dilynwyd gan Winston Churchill. Cynigiwyd swydd i Lloyd George yn y Cabinet Rhyfel, ond yn 77 oed, teimlai na allai ei derbyn. Yn 1944, dychwelodd i fyw gyda'i ail wraig, Frances, ym mhentref ei lencyndod. Yn Ionawr 1945 derbyniodd y 'Great Commoner' iarllaeth. Bu farw ym Mawrth 1945 ac fe'i claddwyd gerllaw'r Afon Ddwyfor.

In the inter-war period Lloyd George, the most dynamic political figure of the time, was forced to stand by, powerless, while lesser men grappled with the problems of depression, unemployment and the breakdown of international order. At the height of the depression he proposed a 'New Deal' for the unemployed, a bold programme of public investment which was rejected by successive governments. Disregarded but feared by those in power, he still remained a figure of adulation in Wales, presiding every year at the National Eisteddfod on the day known as *Diwrnod Lloyd George* (Lloyd George's Day). In the late thirties, however, he withdrew increasingly from the political limelight and spent more and more time on his country estate at Churt in Surrey.

With the growing threat to European peace posed by Nazi Germany in the late thirties, he re-emerged to launch his final campaign. For a brief period Lloyd George, the committed Zionist, had been attracted by Hitler's re-construction of the German economy, but later events, culminating in the Munich crisis, convinced him of the folly of Neville Chamberlain's appeasement policy. With the outbreak of war in 1939, it became evident that Chamberlain had to be replaced. Lloyd George made a forceful intervention in the crucial Commons debate on 8th May 1940:

"I say solemnly that the Prime Minister should give an example of sacrifice, because there is nothing which can contribute more to victory in this war than that he should sacrifice the seals of office."

On 10th May, Chamberlain resigned and was replaced by Winston Churchill. Lloyd George was offered a seat in the War Cabinet, but at the age of 77 he felt unable to accept. In 1944 he returned to live with his second wife, Frances, in his boyhood village. In January 1945 the 'Great Commoner' accepted an earldom. In March 1945 he died and was buried beside the River Dwyfor.

68. 'Bargen Newydd' Lloyd George wedi ei ddarlunio gan *Punch*.

68. Lloyd George's 'New Deal' depicted by *Punch*.

70

71

. Lloyd George, yr 'areithydd' yn yr anialwcholiticaidd, yn y 20au a'r 30au.

. Seremoni Cadeirio y bardd buddugol, Gwenallt,
Eisteddfod Genedlaethol Abertawe, 1926, gyda
loyd George a'r Archdderwydd Elfed, yr emynydd
iwog, yn urddo'r buddugwr. Cynhelid y seremoni
ddydd Iau, 'diwrnod Lloyd George' gyda'i araith
ywyddol yn rhagflaenu'r Cadeirio.

. Lloyd George a sylfaenydd Urdd Gobaith
ymru, Ifan ab Owen Edwards yn croesawu
dward, Tywysog Cymru, yng Nghastell
aernarfon, Mehefin 1934.

69. Lloyd George, 'the orator' in the political
wilderness in the 20s and 30s.

70. The ceremony of the chairing of the victorious
bard, Gwenallt, at the Swansea National Eisteddfod
1926, presided over by Lloyd George and the
Archdruid Elfed the notable Welsh hymn writer.
The ceremony on the Thursday, 'Lloyd George's
Day', was always preceded by his presidential
address.

71. Lloyd George and the founder of Urdd Gobaith
Cymru (The Welsh League of Youth) Ifan ab Owen
Edwards, welcoming Edward, Prince of Wales, at
Caernarfon Castle June 1934.

72

73

72. Lloyd George yn annerch cyfarfod i hyrwyddo achos yr Iddewon yn y 30au cynnar.

73. Lloyd George, a ddenwyd dros dro gan gyfaredd Hitler, gyda'r Unben Natsïaidd yn Berchtesgaden, yn 1936.

74. Lloyd George yn condemnio'n chwyrn Gytundeb Munich â Hitler, a pholisi heddychiad Neville Chamberlain mewn cyfarfod enfawr ym Mhafiliwn y Pier Llandudno, Ionawr 1939. Adroddiad y *Caernarvon and Denbigh Herald*, 20 Ionawr 1939.

75. Lloyd George ym Mhafiliwn y Pier yn areithio'n rymus, gydag E P Evans, Prifathro Ysgol Ramadeg Caernarfon, yn y Gadair.

The European Situa[tion]

"OUTLOOK MORE THREATENING SINCE MUNICH PACT"

Dictators' Fresh and More Startling Demands

MR. LLOYD GEORGE'S LLANDUDNO SPEECH

For more than an hour before Mr. Lloyd George arrived at the Pier Pavilion, Llandudno, last evening, long queues had formed outside the hall which, capable of holding 3,000 people, was packed to its utmost capacity. "I have been present at many political gatherings," writes one reporter, "but never have I seen a demonstration which was more worthy of the description of 'historic'." When he took his place on the platform, the veteran Statesman witnessed an amazing scene. Rank upon rank of his constituents stretched to the back of the hall, every inch of space in the body of the hall and in the balconies being occupied. They had come from town and village, from all parts of the constituency to hear their Member give his views on the international situation—a situation which has steadily grown worse until, at the present time, it is, in Mr. Lloyd George's own words, "full of gravity and menace." It is at such a time of peril, and only a few days after celebrating his 76th birthday, that the ex-Premier selected to expound his views on the international outlook.

. Lloyd George, the Zionist, addressing a [Pr]o-Zionist meeting in the early 30s.

[3]. Lloyd George who was attracted temporarily by [H]itler's charisma, with the Nazi dictator at [Be]rchtesgaden in 1936.

[4]. Lloyd George condemning the Munich pact and [N]eville Chamberlain's appeasement of Hitler at a [pa]cked meeting in the Pier Pavilion Llandudno, [Ja]nuary 1939. Report from the *Caernarvon and [D]enbigh Herald*, 20 January 1939.

[5]. Lloyd George at the Pier Pavilion in fine [o]ratorical flow, with E P Evans, Headmaster of [C]aernarfon Grammar School, in the Chair.

76

77

"You talk as if my affection for you came and went. No more than the sea does because the tide ebbs and flows, there is just as much water in it . . .
"You must make allowances for the waywardness and wildness of a man of my type . . . Believe me hen gariad I am at bottom as fond of you as ever."

Lloyd George to Margaret Lloyd-George (24th July 1924)

"I do not think we have ever loved each other so much. D (avid) says that ours is a love that comes to very few people and I wonder more and more at the beauty and happiness of it. It is a thing that nothing but death can harm and even death has no terror for me, now; for David asked me yesterday if I would come with him when he went."

Frances Stevenson   (Diary, 23rd April 1917)

Bywyd Preifat Private Life

Arweiniodd natur dymhestlog Lloyd George ef i sawl carwriaeth achlysurol. Eto, nid merchetwr cwbl benrhydd mohono. Ei brif gonsyrn oedd gwleidydda, nid mercheta, tra bo dwy gyfathrach bwysicaf ei fywyd o bwysigrwydd dofn a pharhaol iddo.

Bu Margaret Owen, merch yr amaethwr o Fynydd Ednyfed, Criccieth a briododd yn 1888, yn gefnogol-gyson iddo yn ystod ei aml helbulon preifat a chyhoeddus, er gwaetha'r tyndra a nodweddodd eu perthynas yn sgîl ei gyfathrach glos â Frances Stevenson wedi 1912. Gydol ei bywyd, Margaret a fu'n gyfrifol am feithrin ei ganolbwynt grym yn ei etholaeth, Bwrdeisdrefi Arfon, gan gadw ef mewn cysylltiad parhaus â'i wreiddiau.

Bu'n fam i'w pum plentyn, Richard, Mair Eluned, Olwen, Gwilym a Megan. Roedd Lloyd George yn dad gofalus ac ymroddgar, er ei absenoldeb cyson oddi cartref. Roedd yn arbennig o hoff o'i ferched a bu marwolaeth ei ferch hynaf, Mair, yn 17 mlwydd oed, yn 1907, yn loes mawr iddo. Wedi hynny, rhoddodd sylw mawr i'w ferch ieuengaf, Megan (ganwyd 1902) a adlewyrchai yn ei phersonoliaeth fyrlymus a'i dawn wleidyddol, amryw o nodweddion personoliaeth ei thad.

Efallai mai presenoldeb Megan a sicrhaodd barhâd priodas Margaret a David Lloyd George fel cyfathrach bwysig ac ystyriol, hyd yn oed yn y 1920au a'r 30au, pan yr oedd ef yn byw ym Mron y De, Churt, Swydd Surrey, tra arhosai Margaret am gyfnodau maith ym Mryn Awelon, Criccieth. Pan y bu farw Margaret yn 1941, llethwyd ef gan dristwch oherwydd bu'n gymar cyson a ffyddlon iddo ac yn fam ardderchog i'w plant, er holl dymestl eu priodas.

Lloyd George's tempestuous nature undoubtedly led him into several casual affairs. Yet, he was no unrestrained libertine. His prime concern was politics, not philandering, while the two meaningful relationships of his life were of an enduring and vital importance to him.

Margaret Owen, the farmer's daughter of Mynydd Ednyfed, Criccieth, whom he married in 1888, remained a steadfast source of support for him during the frequent public and private vicissitudes he endured, despite the strains which affected their relationship following his growing involvement with Frances Stevenson after 1912. Margaret maintained his power base in his Caernarfon Boroughs constituency throughout her lifetime and kept him in touch with the grass roots from which he had sprung.

She also bore him 5 children, Richard, Mair Eluned, Olwen, Gwilym and Megan. Lloyd George was a caring and devoted father, in spite of his frequent absences from home. He was particularly attached to his daughters and was moved to intense grief when his eldest daughter Mair died at 17 years of age in 1907. He then lavished his attention upon his youngest daughter, Megan (born 1902), whose political gifts and vivacious personality reflected so many features of her father's character.

It was perhaps Megan's presence which ensured that Margaret and David Lloyd George's marriage remained a deep and compassionate relationship, even in the 1920s and 1930s, when he lived at Bron y De, Churt, in Surrey, while his wife preferred to remain for lengthly periods at Bryn Awelon, Criccieth. When she died in 1941, Lloyd

78
Gwilym, Mair, Richard, Olwen
Mrs Lloyd George, Megan

Cyfathrach holl bwysig arall ei fywyd oedd ei berthynas hir-hoedlog â Frances Stevenson. Yn 1911 fe'i penodwyd hi yn athrawes Ffrangeg dros-dro ar Megan. Erbyn 1912 daeth yn ysgrifenyddes ac yn feistres iddo, a gweddill ei fywyd Frances oedd un o'i gynghorwyr politicaidd pwysicaf. Yn ferch hardd a thra phenderfynol bu'n gefn iddo gydol tryblith a phryderon ei brif weinidogaeth ryfel ac yn ystod ei gyfnod hir yn y diffeithwch politicaidd ar ôl 1922, parhaodd i'w ysbrydoli i estyn ei ddylanwad mawr o'r cyrion ar wleidyddiaeth Prydain. Yn 1929 esgorodd ar Jennifer. 'Roedd Lloyd George yn dotio arni. Galwai hi ef 'Taid'. Yn 1943, priodwyd Frances a Lloyd George ac yn ddiweddarach yn 1945, dyrchafwyd hi yn Iarlles Lloyd George o Ddwyfor. Parodd perthynas Lloyd George â Frances ddrwgdeimlad mawr rhwng Frances a theulu Lloyd George.

Eto, ni ellir gwadu na fu Margaret a Frances, yn eu ffyrdd gwahanol, yn swcwr a chryfder iddo i gynnal ei ymgysegriad hir i'w briod nod mewn bywyd – gwleidyddiaeth – a'i frwdfrydedd parhaus dros gyfiawnder cymdeithasol.

Bu ei frawd, William, o gymorth mawr iddo hefyd. Ef a fu'n ysgwyddo'r baich o gynnal eu busnes cyfreithiol yng Ngogledd Cymru, gan sicrhau cymorth ariannol i'r AS ifanc, cymharol dlawd. Ef, hefyd, a'i achubodd rhag helyntion personol ac ariannol enbyd yn ystod ei yrfa gynnar. Ar ôl marwolaeth Uncle Lloyd yn 1917, ymgynghorai'n aml â William, pan yr oedd angen cyngor

79. Margaret, Megan, David Lloyd George. 1919

80　　　　81

80. Jennifer, merch Frances Stevenson, gyda'i mam.

81. Lloyd George gyda Jennifer a'i galwai'n 'Taid'.

82. Gyda'i ferch ieuengaf, Megan.

George was stricken by grief, for Margaret had been a constant and faithful wife, and caring mother, despite their turbulent marriage.

The other profound relationship of his life was with Frances Stevenson. In 1911 she had been appointed as a temporary governess to teach French to Megan. By 1912 she had become his secretary and mistress and for the remainder of his life she was one of his closest political advisers. A woman of great determination and beauty, she guided him through the stresses and strains of his Wartime Premiership and during his long sojourn in the political wilderness after 1922 she continued to inspire him to seek to exert profound political influence from the sidelines. In 1929 she gave birth to Jennifer. Lloyd George doted upon her, while she called him 'Taid'. In 1943 Frances became Lloyd George's wife and subsequently the Countess Lloyd George of Dwyfor in 1945.

Lloyd George's relationship with Frances undoubtedly caused considerable friction between Frances and his family. Yet both Margaret and Frances, in their different ways, gave him the succour and strength he required to sustain him in his lifelong dedication to his major love – politics – and his constant quest for social justice.

His brother William also proved to be a consistent source of strength to him. He not only carried the burden of maintaining their solicitor's business in North Wales, thus ensuring financial support for the impecunious young MP, but he also saved him from grave per-

80. Jennifer, daughter of Frances Stevenson, with her mother.

81. Lloyd George with Jennifer, who called him 'Taid' (Grandfather).

82. With his youngest daughter, Megan.

doeth a gofalus.

Pan y câi Lloyd George gyfle i ymlacio ac ymbellhau o gynnwrf gwleidydda, ei hoff ddileit oedd chwarae golff. Mwynhâi bysgota, hefyd, a hoffai broffesu diddordeb mewn gwersylla. Ei hoffder mwyaf, fodd bynnag, oedd teithio a gydol ei yrfa ymwelodd â mannau estron egsotig fel Nice, Cannes ac amryw ganolfannau twristaidd eraill hudolus yn Ne Ffrainc, yn ogystal ag ymweid ag America, Canada, Ynysoedd y Caribî, yr Eidal a Phatagonia.

Ar ôl 1921, pan brynodd Bron y De, Churt, Swydd Surrey, trodd ei egnïon i gyfeiriad garddio a ffarmio. Daeth yn enwog fel tyfwr ffrwythau, yn enwedig mefus a mafon; agorodd Siop Stad yn Churt i werthu'r cynnyrch ac enillodd wobrau niferus mewn sioeau garddio. Enillodd glod hefyd fel bridiwr moch a gwenynwr. Roedd hefyd yn hoff iawn o gerdded a mynd a'i gŵn am dro. Adlewyrchai ei ddiddordebau hamdden ei wreiddiau gwledig, gwerinol, er bod ei hoffder o ysmygu ambell sigar a blasu gwydriad o 'whisky' yn achlysurol, yn ystod cyfnod diweddaraf ei oes, yn dadlennu gwrthgyferbyniadau parhaus ei bersonoliaeth gymhleth.

83.

84.

85.

86.

83. Golffio yng Nghricieth gyda Syr Rufus Isaacs a C F G Masterman, 1911.

84. Gwersylla gyda'i deulu ar lethrau Moel Hebog.

85. Glanio yn Dover, ar ôl gwyliau yn yr Eidal, Mai 1922.

86. Croeso mawr yn 10, Stryd Downing ar yr un achlysur, Mai 1922. Ar y chwith iddo, mae ei unig nai, W R P George.

87. Gwyliau yn y Cannes, Ionawr 1922, gyda Frances (rhes gefn dde), a Tom Jones, Ysgrifennydd y Cabinet, (rhes gefn chwith).

sonal and financial scandals during his early career. After the death of Uncle Lloyd in 1917, William was often consulted when sound and measured advice was required.

Away from the turmoil of politics, Lloyd George's favourite relaxation was golf. He also enjoyed camping. His greatest delight, however, was travelling and throughout his life he visited exotic and luxurious areas, not only Nice, Cannes and other salubrious resorts in the South of France which he particularly enjoyed, but also America, Canada, the West Indies, Italy and Patagonia.

From 1921 onwards, when he bought Bron y De, Churt, in Surrey, he devoted much energy to market gardening. He became renowned as a cultivator of fruits, particularly strawberries and raspberries; he opened an estate shop at Churt to sell his produce, and won numerous prizes at gardening shows. He also became a highly successful beekeeper and pig breeder. He took great pleasure, too, in walking and exercising his dogs. His pastimes had much of the rural flavour of a man drawn from peasant stock, although his penchant for cigars and, in the latter period of his life, his partiality for an occasional whisky and some champagne, did reveal the ever parodoxical features of his personality.

83. Golfing at Criccieth with Sir Rufus Isaacs and C F G Masterman, 1911.

84. Camping with his family on the slopes of Moel Hebog.

85. Disembarking at Dover after an Italian holiday, May 1922.

86. A great welcome at 10 Downing Street on the same occasion, May 1922. On his left his 'only little nephew' W R P George.

87. A holiday at Cannes, January 1922, with Frances (back row right) and Tom Jones, Cabinet Secretary (back row left).

88

89

90

88. Y garddwr yn Churt.

89. Y ffarmwr yn Churt, gyda Frances.

90. Yn Churt, Nadolig 1936, yn diddanu plant gweithwyr ei fferm.

91. 1936, Churt, gyda Dai y Corgi, Mŵg a Groc.

88. The gardener at Churt.

89. The farmer at Churt, with Frances.

90. At Churt, Christmas 1936, entertaining the children of his farmworkers.

91. 1936, Churt, with Dai the corgi, Mŵg and Groc.

92. Ymgom gyda phentrefwr ar y bont yn Llanystumdwy, 1940, gyda'r Fonesig Margaret yn y cefndir.

93. Lloyd George gyda'r Iarlles wrth y Bont, yn Llanystumdwy, yn 1945 wythnosau prin cyn ei farwolaeth.

A chat with a villager on the bridge at
Llanystumdwy, 1940, with Dame Margaret in the
background.

Lloyd George with the Countess at the Old
Bridge, Llanystumdwy, in 1945 shortly before his
death.

94. Y portread olaf gyda Frances, 1945.

94. The last portrait, with Frances, 1945.

95. Ei frawd, William, ar achlysur ei ben-blwydd yn 100 oed, gerllaw cerflun David Lloyd George, ar y Maes, Caernarfon.

95. His brother, William, on his 100th birthday, near David Lloyd George's statue, Castle Square, Caernarfon.